# THE KEYS TO SUCCESS IN MANAGEMENT

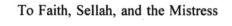

To Faith, Sellah, and the Mistress

# The Keys to Success in Management

HENRY KYAMBALESA
*School of Business, Copperbelt University*

Routledge
Taylor & Francis Group

LONDON AND NEW YORK

First published 1998 by Ashgate Publishing

Reissued 2018 by Routledge
2 Park Square, Milton Park, Abingdon, Oxon, OX14 4RN
711 Third Avenue, New York, NY 10017, USA

*Routledge is an imprint of the Taylor & Francis Group, an informa business*

Notice:
Product or corporate names may be trademarks or registered trademarks, and are used only for identification and explanation without intent to infringe.

Publisher's Note
The publisher has gone to great lengths to ensure the quality of this reprint but points out that some imperfections in the original copies may be apparent.

Disclaimer
The publisher has made every effort to trace copyright holders and welcomes correspondence from those they have been unable to contact.

A Library of Congress record exists under LC control number: 98030176

ISBN 13: 978-1-138-34910-0 (hbk)
ISBN 13: 978-0-429-43643-7 (ebk)

# CONTENTS

<>

# LIST OF FIGURES AND TABLES

<>

# PREFACE

To become a manager in an organisational setting is, no doubt, an enormous achievement for individuals who have a desire to play a greater role in shaping the destiny of their organisations. Thus, a managerial job can be a potential source of great exhilaration and excitement for individuals who have a craving for it and are adequately prepared to wrestle with the challenges and onerous responsibilities of the job.

However, becoming a manager can also be a source of distress and anxiety, particularly for people who may not have sufficient managerial knowledge and skills. This book is designed to provide a stimulating discourse on the requisite knowledge, skills and drive which prospective and practising managers need to possess if they are to enjoy discharging the duties of the managerial job, as well as contribute positively to the long-term success and survival of their organisations. Specifically, the following themes are explored in the book: (1) the management process; (2) business communication; (3) organisational competitiveness; (4) dealings with external parties; (5) self-management; and (6) rethinking Western management.

As we proceed to explore *The Keys to Success in Management*, let us keep in mind the following caveat adopted from Price Pritchett's *New Work Habits for a Radically Changing World*:

> *Expect your [organisation] ... to expect more from you. The reason? The marketplace is demanding far more these days from the organisation itself. Clients and customers want much better quality than before ... [t]hey expect top-notch service, too, or they'll take their business to your competitors.*[1]

H.K., DENVER, USA                                     SEPTEMBER 1998

ix

# THE KEYS TO SUCCESS IN MANAGEMENT

# 1/ THE MANAGEMENT PROCESS

*Visualisation of a task to be performed is ... funda-*
*mental to the successful execution of the task.*[2]

Let us start here by defining the term "management." As a *process*,
the term essentially refers to the generation of organisational units and
the coordination and integration of the units and available resources
to accomplish specified targets and objectives. However, it should be
noted that the term is also alternately used to refer to the *discipline*
concerned with understanding and improving the knowledge and skills
in managing an organisation, or the *group of persons* that is charged
with the responsibility for managing the affairs and resources of an
organisation.

Management, as a process, enjoys wide application. In organisational settings, it is employed at literally all levels (that is, top, middle
and lower levels of management), and in various functional units (that
is, accounting, finance, marketing, personnel, production, and other
units). In society, management is apparently applied by all kinds of
organisations. And across societies, management occupies a prominent
niche regardless of the nature of prevailing socio-economic systems
or ideological differences.

This chapter is devoted to a survey of the following elements of
the management process: the management functions, managerial decision-making, human resource management, and labour-management
relations. An understanding of these elements should, by and large,
enable us to visualise the nitty gritty of the managerial job.

In the interim, let us remember that managerial competence is not

1

an in-born quality or attribute; rather, it is acquired through learning. However, one cannot learn to become an effective manager entirely from books, lectures, seminars, and workshops; many aspects of managerial competence, as Glueck has maintained,[3] are learnt best in practice. Therefore, those who aspire to become competent managers need to learn as much from books, lectures, seminars, and/or work- shops as from practice. And, obviously, the onus for such "learning" lies squarely upon each and every individual who wishes to become a successful manager, as Pritchett has advised:

> *Life-long learning is the only way to remain competi- tive in the job market. You should invest in your own growth, development, and self-renewal.*[4]

It should be noted, though, that management knowledge and skills are not permanent acquisitions at all; unless they are constantly enriched and replenished with current thinking, they can eventually become less potent or even inept. There are many factors in the decision maker's environment that are likely to depreciate the efficacy of acquired management knowledge and skills. One such factor pertains to changes in ideas, work methods and procedures, and machinery and equipment. A manager who is effective with a particular *modus operandi*, for example, may not be as effective when his or her organisation adopts a new way of doing things.

Another important factor concerns memory decay. With the passage of time, decision makers are very likely to be less knowledge- able and skilful if they cannot keep abreast with new knowledge and ideas in their fields of endeavour. To be able to maintain the neces- sary management knowledge and skills, therefore, managers need to read widely and, among other things, attend management seminars and workshops on a regular basis. If they cannot find time for updating their knowledge and skills, they should not wonder when they become less potent in their managerial pursuits and endeavours and eventually become a liability to their organisations.

[*Nota bene*: The term "manager" is used in this book to refer to any organisational member in any field of specialisation who is res- ponsible for performing the management tasks or functions discussed in the ensuing section. Therefore, engineers, church leaders, army officers, foremen, physicians, entrepreneurs, professors, sports coaches, government ministers, and all other kinds of office bearers are essentially managers in the institutions they serve.]

## 1.1 THE MANAGEMENT FUNCTIONS

Certain tasks need to be performed if the management effort is to yield any desirable outcomes; these tasks may be conveniently grouped in two categories as follows: *classical management functions*, and *Mintzberg's managerial roles*. According to classical management theory, the management process is accomplished through the performance of the functions or tasks of planning, organising, directing, and controlling. The first function, that is, *planning*, involves the following: (a) charting the mission or overall long-range direction of an organisation; (b) formulating specific short-, medium-, and long-range objectives; (c) determining policies and procedures; and (d) developing operational plans. The planning function rests upon the mental capacities of the planner and the adequacy and accuracy of information needed for planning. Experience and intelligent vision and judgment are among mental tools that business planners need to possess.

*Organising*, as a function of management, simply refers to the arrangement of individuals, materials, machines, and other resources into the best possible relationships that will facilitate the attainment of stipulated goals. It involves the following: (a) developing a formal structure for the organisation; (b) grouping activities into departments or sections; (c) defining the span of control for each managerial and supervisory position; (d) specifying relationships between and among work units with respect to lines of authority, responsibility, and accountability; and (e) delegating the necessary authority and responsibility to those who are expected to perform specified tasks.

*Directing*, the third function of management, involves the following: (a) integrating the needs of individual employees with those of the business organisation; (b) motivating employees so that they can willingly invest their time, energies and commitment toward achieving stipulated goals; and (c) providing direction for all employees by means of effective communication.

The fourth function of management, that is, *controlling*, serves two primary purposes, that is, evaluating the nature of activities taking place within a given organisational setting and fine-tuning the operation of the business organisation to achieve superior results. These two purposes can be accomplished by means of the following six distinct steps: (a) observation of employees' performance; (b) determination of performance standards; (c) measurement of actual performance; (d) determination of deviations of actual performance from specified standards; (e) investigation of causes of slack performance; and (f) taking the necessary corrective measures when there are deviations.[5] A diagrammatic representation of these steps is provided in Figure 1.1. Each of the six steps is briefly discussed below.

Figure 1.1:   The Control Process

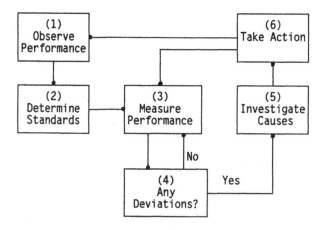

1) OBSERVATION OF PERFORMANCE.   In this first step, managers should carefully observe the performance of the people they oversee. This step is perhaps a critical one when the activities to be controlled are new to an organisation. Employees' performance should be monitored and their maximum and minimum output recorded regularly for at least one year. The objective here should be to determine the average output per person per time period. The output may be measured in

terms of items produced or sold, files processed, customers contacted, or any other possible means of measuring performance.

2) DETERMINATION OF STANDARDS. Observation of employees' performance should lead to the determination of performance standards, that is, the optimal levels of performance each and every employee's performance needs to be measured against. Ideally, performance standards should be realistic and achievable. They should be set in view of human capabilities, external and internal conditions, and resources available. Standards that are set arbitrarily without considering human capabilities and prevailing circumstances may turn out to be a source of frustration among employees resulting from failure of accomplishment.

3) MEASUREMENT OF PERFORMANCE. Once performance standards are determined and communicated to each and every employee, the next step should be to measure employees' actual performance. This has to be done to facilitate the determination of whether or not organisational members are each contributing what is expected of them. Unless employees' actual performance is measured, the next step in the control process - that is, the determination of deviations - cannot be prosecuted at all.

4) DETERMINATION OF DEVIATIONS. At this step, an executive needs to compare employees' actual performance with performance standards to determine whether there are any deviations. See Table 1.1 for an illustration of the determination of deviations. The information in this Table shows us that, in one particular week, Sam, Jim, and Dick sold 50, 200, and 150 units less than the weekly standard of 1,500 units, respectively. Noel, however, sold 100 units in excess of the set standard. (It is assumed here that the sales potential is the same throughout the organisation's four sales territories.)

To determine what to do next, the following question should be asked about the performance of each employee: Does it significantly deviate from the specified standard? If the answer is "no," return to the previous step and measure the performance for the next period. If it is "yes," move to the next step and investigate the possible causes of the deviation.

5) STUDY OF CAUSES OF DEVIATIONS. A careful and thorough investigation of the causes of deviations of employees' performance from the stipulated standards should be made in order to take or prescribe appropriate remedial measures. Some possible causes could be the following: (a) unrealistic standards (that is, standards that are either too high or too low); (b) inadequate resources (such as finance, support personnel, materials, time, and equipment) available to personnel; or (c) environmental factors (such as competition, economic conditions, and political influences).

6) TAKING REMEDIAL ACTION. Once the causes of deviations are identified, the next step should be to take the necessary corrective measures. For example, if it is discovered that the standards are too high for an average employee to attain, move to the first step (see Figure 1.1) and observe performance again to be able to set new, more realistic performance standards. Sometimes the standards may be lower than employees are able to attain; this would also call for a return to the first step to observe performance and then determine more realistic standards.

Table 1.1:  Determining Deviations

| Salesman | Sales territory | Standard in unit sales per week | Actual sales in units per week | Deviations in units |
|----------|-----------------|---------------------------------|--------------------------------|---------------------|
| 1. Sam | A | 1,500 | 1,450 | (50) |
| 2. Jim | B | 1,500 | 1,300 | (200) |
| 3. Noel | C | 1,500 | 1,600 | 100 |
| 4. Dick | D | 1,500 | 1,350 | (150) |

If the causes pertain to inadequate resources, however, more of such resources should be made available and then return to the third step and measure the performance for the next period of time. The next several steps - that is, steps 4, 5 and 6 - should be followed all over again.

MINTZBERG'S MANAGERIAL ROLES. In contrast to the functions of management espoused by classical theorists, Henry Mintzberg, on the basis of his study of the activities of managers in various kinds of organisations, has described the typical manager's job in terms of ten functional roles, which he has classified under three categories as follows: interpersonal roles, informational roles, and decision-related roles. The specific roles which fall under each of these categories are described in a nutshell in the ensuing paragraphs.

INTERPERSONAL ROLES. (1) representing a business or organisational entity on ceremonial and other occasions - the "figurehead" role; (2) motivating and supervising employees, and exercising formal authority within their business organisations - the "leader" role; and (3) interacting with other managers and groups outside one's organisational entity - the "liaison" role.

INFORMATIONAL ROLES. (1) transmitting various kinds of information to organisational members - the "disseminator" role; (2) collecting and receiving both internal and external information concerning the organisation - the "monitor" role; and (3) informing outside parties about the business entity's activities - the "spokesman" role.

DECISION-RELATED ROLES. (1) taking charge when crises resulting from internal or external forces arise - the "disturbance handler" role; (2) initiating changes in order to cope with internal and external forces - the "innovator" role; (3) dealing with situations involving business-related negotiations with external parties - the "negotiator" role; and (4) deciding where organisational efforts, energies and resources are to be directed to achieve greater efficiency and productivity - the "resource allocator" role.[6]

## 1.2 DECISION MAKING

The term "decision making" refers to the process of selecting from a set of alternatives the best possible alternative that will forestall a given problem or attain a desired state of being. Ideally, the outcome of the decision-making process (that is, managerial decisions) should be completely rational. However, rationality is not usually tenable in practice owing to lack of perfect knowledge about available decision choices and the consequences of decision choices, among a host of other things.

The managerial decision-making process essentially consists of the following steps: (a) setting goals to be achieved in a given period of time or diagnosing existing and/or potential problems;[7] (b) searching for or consideration of alternative goals and/or solutions; (c) evaluation and comparison of the alternative goals and/or solutions; (d) selection of the best goal and/or most feasible decision choice; (e) setting out to achieve the stipulated goal and/or implementation of the selected decision alternative; and (f) making the necessary follow-up and institution of control measures to ensure that business activities are performed as planned.[8]

Some situations in the decision maker's world require subordinates' involvement in the identification of problems or opportunities, search for decision alternatives, evaluation and comparison of alternatives, selection of the best alternative, and so on. For example, a manager who has a work force consisting of competent and technically or professionally qualified employees cannot possibly diagnose existing and/or potential problems and make effective decisions alone. Therefore, business managers also need to develop an aptitude in engaging employees or subordinates in the decision-making process.

Group participation in decision making may occur in any one of the following two ways or both (in most cases both): through committees, and/or through loosely defined or spontaneously formed groups of subordinates. A variant to group and committee problem diagnosis and decision making is the use of suggestion systems or gripe boxes, which can be used by employees to anonymously suggest ways in which an organisation's overall performance and productivity can be improved.[9]

Both group and committee problem diagnosis and decision making require good relations among managers and the rank and file, that is, a state of interpersonal relationships that has the potential to bring about high levels of understanding and cooperation between and among individuals in a business setting. Simply stated, the term is used to refer to organisational members' ability to work harmoniously with each other in their pursuit of stipulated goals.

In any given organisational setting, most tasks are accomplished through deliberate interactions between and among groups of people. And, as many of us may have observed, task accomplishment in all organisational settings is deeply rooted in cooperation and understanding between and among members of work groups. Similarly, failure to accomplish tasks is, in the majority of cases, a direct result of poor relations. Stated more succinctly, task accomplishment in any given organisational setting is not possible unless there are harmonious relations between business managers and the various parties they interact with in their business pursuits.

Managers, therefore, need to develop a skill in dealing harmoniously with employees and other parties, because lack of the human relations skill on their part can result in scepticism, bickering, divided purposes, indifference, and frustration at work - the culmination of which can be detrimental to the success and survival of an organisation. Basically, the human relations skill requires that business managers possess such qualities as the following: a mature disposition, emotional stability, personal drive, and, among other things, impartiality.

Before we proceed to the next section, let us review the following important aspects pertaining to decision making: pre-conditions for decision making, decision-making situations, attitude toward risk, environmental and personal factors in decision making, technical and computer skills, and a corporate vision.

1) PRE-CONDITIONS FOR DECISION MAKING. The following preconditions should normally exist for any decision making to take place: (a) there should be a gap between the present situation and the desired state of being; (b) the decision maker should be aware of the gap; (c) the decision maker should have the necessary level of motivation to reduce the gap; and (d) there should be adequate resources within the decision maker's reach to enable him or her do something about the gap.[10]

2) DECISION-MAKING SITUATIONS. Under competitive market conditions,

business managers make decisions in situations of certainty, risk and uncertainty. In situations of certainty, decision makers have perfect knowledge about available decision alternatives and their consequences, with no element of chance intervening between an alternative and its outcome. Decisions are made under conditions of risk when decision makers know the available decision alternatives but cannot ascertain the exact outcomes or consequences of the alternatives.

Most managerial decisions are made under conditions of risk. Under conditions of uncertainty, the decision maker does not know the available decision choices and their possible outcomes or consequences - this usually occurs when a decision maker is faced with a completely new problem or situation for which no information or data are available.[11]

3) ATTITUDE TOWARD RISK.[12] In terms of their attitude toward risk, decision makers can be classified as follows: (a) those who prefer risky decisions and business pursuits (risk seekers); (b) those who try by all means to avoid risk (risk averters); and (c) those who are generally indifferent to risk. By and large, decision makers may be characterised as being risk averters by nature.

4) ENVIRONMENTAL FACTORS. When making decisions, business managers must usually consider a host of factors external to their business entities that are likely to make their decisions less potent, such as political influences, competition, customers' perceptions and attitudes, labour union demands and expectations, and the like. Unless such factors are considered, any decisions made cannot possibly result in desired outcomes.

5) PERSONAL FACTORS. There are many individual-based factors that affect the quality of a business manager's decisions; they include one's beliefs, personal values, attitude toward risk (briefly described above), and level of education. In terms of attitude toward risk, for example, an executive who is indifferent to risk is likely to choose a riskier decision alternative even when such an alternative is not expected to yield better results than less risky alternatives.

6) TECHNICAL AND COMPUTER SKILLS. The term "technical skill" is

applied here to refer to an individual's ability to perform specific kinds of activities in a specialised field of work. The activities referred to here include techniques, methods, and procedures. Technical skills are essential for increasing the efficiency and effectiveness of production operations.[13] An engineer, for example, should possess all the necessary knowledge and skills required of him to perform effectively in his specialised field of endeavour. Also, a physician needs to have specialised knowledge and skills pertaining to his kind of field.

Closely related to the technical skill just described is an aptitude in using, as well as a flare to use, computers. We now live in the "computer age." This is common sense, at least among most managers. Unfortunately, there are still some managers who do not appreciate fully what the computer can do and what it cannot do for them. The computer is among those tools which today's business managers cannot possibly dispense with if they are to be effective in their pursuits and endeavours.

This does not, of course, imply that the computer can do what managers themselves cannot do - not at all! The computer only does better, faster, and more reliably what decision makers can also do. And since it is inanimate, it does not get tired, nor does it forget or claim overtime. Additionally, the costs of storing data as well as those of computation associated with the computer are only a tiny fraction of the costs involved in the absence of a computer.

In other words, the computer can greatly enhance the ability and the effectiveness of decision makers. Decision makers, therefore, need to get acquainted with the uses and operation of computers. If they cannot do this, they will continue to wrestle with figures, computations, and data processing even when they have a computer which can do these and other activities faster and more accurately.

7) CORPORATE VISION. Modern organisations need managers who are generally savvy regarding the various aspects and facets of management - staffing, marketing, strategic management, financial management, and, among other things, public relations and social responsibility. A person whose training, knowledge and skills are confined to only one or so aspects of management would, therefore, be like the proverbial "square peg in a round hole" in a managerial job. Unless managers strive to gain a clear understanding of the overall workings

of their organisational entities, therefore, they are not likely to marshall the human, material, and other resources under their charge in an effective manner.

This should be obvious because a manager who has superficial knowledge about his or her organisation and the various elements of its external environment is not likely to make effective decisions; if anything, such a manager is, at best, a liability to his or her organisation. As such, managers need to have a clear understanding of how the units and functions of their organisations depend on one another and how changes in one unit can affect the other units. And, among a host of other things, they need to develop an aptitude in assessing, as well as mitigating, the negative impacts of their decisions and activities on society at large.

## 1.3  HUMAN RESOURCE MANAGEMENT

The term "human resource management," or "staffing," may be defined to refer to an organisational function or process whose purpose is to provide and retain competent human resources a business entity needs to be able to bolster its operations. Essentially, the process encompasses the following elements: human resource planning, employee acquirement, remuneration, performance appraisals, maintenance of discipline among employees, and training and development.[14]

Skilful management of the staffing function can enable an executive to hire and retain talented people who have the potential to contribute meaningfully to the success and survival of his or her business. It is, therefore, incumbent upon business executives to gain a thorough understanding of the basic elements of the human resource management process if they are to steer their businesses to success. Brief descriptions of the elements of the process of human resource management follow in the ensuing paragraphs.

HUMAN RESOURCE PLANNING.  This element of the staffing function basically involves the following activities: forecasting a business's future human resource needs, comparing the business's current work force and its future personnel needs to determine the numbers and types of people who need to be hired or phased out in order to maintain an optimal number of personnel, and job prescription.

The third task, that is, "job prescription," becomes necessary only when a new job position is created, and should involve the following: (a) defining the nature of the job - that is, providing a clear and concise description of what is expected of the job holder in terms of responsibilities and accountabilities, as well as the authority he or she is expected to assume; and (b) stipulating the necessary attributes the job holder is expected to possess, such as skills, knowledge, experience, and/or any other attributes that are important in performing the job.

PERSONNEL ACQUIREMENT.[15] Essentially, this element of the human resource management process requires business managers to sequentially perform the following tasks: recruitment, selection, and orientation of employees. The first task, that is, *recruitment*, involves sourcing, contacting, and attracting qualified job applicants to fill a vacancy or job opening. Following recruitment is the *selection* process, which may typically include the following steps:

a) Completion, by job applicants, of an application blank, the purpose of which should be to obtain the relevant details and particulars about each applicant, including his or her referees, level of education and vocational training, length of relevant experience, physical characteristics, and hobbies and interests;

b) Screening out job applicants whose aptitudes or qualifications are not consistent with those stipulated by management;

c) Making reference and background checks on applicants who successfully make it through the preceding step;

d) Conducting an in-depth interview with each applicant to gain more insights about his or her suitability for employment;

e) Evaluation of the physical and/or medical examination results for applicants who successfully go through the foregoing step; and

f) Making the decision to hire, or not to hire, the job applicant or applicants who may successfully make it through the fifth step.

*Orientation.* This is the last step in the personnel acquirement process; it is intended to ensure that job applicants who are recruited and selected for employment are officially introduced to various important aspects and facets of their new work environment, including the rules and regulations they are expected to observe, the realm and scope of their work, and their job positions' authority relationships with other positions and work groups in the business undertaking.

REMUNERATION OF EMPLOYEES. This involves making decisions concerning the appropriate forms and combinations of employee compensation. The various types of remuneration which an executive may consider include wages, salaries, fringe benefits, periodic bonuses, overtime pay, and profit sharing. One may, for example, consider a performance-based remuneration package for regular employees consisting of the following: (a) basic pay, which all employees should be entitled to except when they take an unauthorised leave of absence; (b) hourly rate; (c) overtime pay for, say, over forty hours of work per week; and (d) a 1% raise in basic pay upon every favourable performance review.

PERFORMANCE APPRAISAL. This is basically a periodic evaluation of how well employees are discharging their duties, the ultimate purposes of which may include the following: (a) to determine each employee's readiness for promotion; (b) to determine whether or not some employees need training or re-training; and (c) to determine whether or not an employee's performance is good enough to warrant a salary raise or special inducements intended to lure him or her from prospective employers. Besides, performance assessments can partly provide information needed in performance improvement planning, as well as enable a manager to generate the necessary documentation on each employee which may be used in the business's employee-related dealings with labour unions, governmental agencies and/or other external parties.[16]

A major requirement in performance appraisals is the use of observable and/or measurable evaluation criteria. Moreover, the criteria to be used need to be related to an employee's job. And, if they are to be fair, performance appraisals need to be discussed with employees involved. This should be done if employees are to be afforded the opportunity to vindicate themselves if they wish to; in fact, this can also provide an opportunity for employees to discuss their strengths and weaknesses with their bosses and enable them to identify areas in which they need to improve.

CHECKING INDISCIPLINE. This aspect of staffing requires an employer to devise a disciplinary code, that is, a set of rules which employees are expected to observe, including time, safety and insubordination rules, as well as specific disciplinary actions which should be expected to be taken if and when an employee breaks the stipulated rules or regulations.

TRAINING AND DEVELOPMENT. This is essentially a formally instituted programme designed to ensure that employees' knowledge and skills are continually improved and upgraded through seminars, in-house training, workshops, refresher courses, and on-the-job training. The ultimate purpose of such a programme is to reap the benefits which are generally associated with having a sufficiently skilled and knowledgeable work force; these include the following: improved quality and quantity of a business's product offerings, and a reduction in both waste and accidents at places of work. James Renier has succinctly summed up the subject: "If we help people develop into the best they can become ... we will get the innovation and productivity we seek."[17]

*Conclusion.* In all, it is essential for executives to remember the fact that human beings - anywhere and everywhere - are not perfect at all; they have mental, physical, and other weaknesses and limitations which can have an adverse effect on their levels of performance and productivity. It is, therefore, only prudent to learn to harness fully the potential of human resources to contribute positively to the success and survival of one's business by working within the confines of their inherent weaknesses and limitations.

And, as Blanchard and Johnson have advised,[18] every manager needs to take a minute out of each of his or her work days to look into the faces of employees and to realise that they are his or her most important resources. Managers who cannot discern the need to embrace this tenet would do well to consider a career in, say, wildlife management.

For an executive who manages a diverse work force, it is essential to be sensitive to such issues as those concerning employees' race, ethnic origin, religious affiliation, gender, and physical disabilities, as well as develop a skill in dealing successfully with these issues. Additionally, executives need to avoid employment practices that are based on such factors as race, colour, gender, religious affiliation, and ethnic extraction.

Further, it is essential to furnish employees with safety and health regulations, which should stipulate potential health hazards in the work place, and safety procedures for handling and storing hazardous materials and/or equipment. Besides, there is a need to provide protective clothing and/or equipment to employees whose jobs expose them to potentially hazardous situations. All these efforts need to be accompanied by a formal training programme designed to educate employees about their obligations, the obligations of the employer, and any other important matters and guidelines concerning occupational safety and health.

One would, of course, be amiss to discuss personnel matters and issues without reminding managers about their responsibility to safeguard each and every employee's right to privacy, particularly with respect to medical records, income, and any other sensitive and personal matters which individuals would naturally expect their managers to keep with strict confidentiality.[19]


## 1.4 LABOUR-MANAGEMENT RELATIONS

The presence of organised labour in an organisational setting creates two institutions within one organisation between which employees have to divide their allegiance. Since the existence and success of any labour union generally depends on convincing its members - at least by implication - that management is their arch enemy, the rank and file in unionised organisations naturally tend to identify themselves more with the goals and aspirations of their representative unions. Needless to say, this tends to make unionised workers less concerned about the need for their employer-organisations to attain protracted growth and greater efficiency.

There is no doubt that this kind of attitude among workers can culminate in organisational failure and consequently result in loss of employment. In their dealings with workers and labour unions, therefore, managers need to be wary of decisions, actions and programmes that are likely to evoke undesirable incidents like strikes and go-slows. And during collective bargaining, employers should always insist on active and genuine dialogue. Further, they need to avoid undue delays when exploring the feasibility of meeting union demands.

Perhaps a more prudent and tactical approach for an organisation's management should be to cater, in collaboration with a representative union, for the welfare of workers without having to wait for the union to table workers' demands. After all, employers generally know what constitutes a livable wage under any given economic conditions. A voluntary posture toward the welfare of employees, although it can very easily undermine employees' rationale for union representation in an organisation, can greatly mitigate the incidence of labour strife.

It is also important for employers to guard against the temptation to take advantage of warnings that may be sounded by governments and/or the judiciary in their countries of operation that stern measures would be taken against workers who uncompromisingly resort to strike action as a means of getting their demands met. They should not use such warnings to fortify their positions in bargaining even when workers' demands are justified. In general, managers, as Ephlin has advised, need to conceive of labour unions more as partners in achieving organisational success and survival than as their formidable enemy.[20]

<>

# 2/ BUSINESS COMMUNICATION

*Poor ... [communication] turns first impression into
lasting bad impression.*[21]

Good communication skills are an indispensable factor in the success
of any given manager - and of any individual whose work requires
him or her to have regular interactions with people, as a matter of
fact. But like any other element or factor in the manager's arsenal of
aptitudes, the communication skill is not an in-born quality or
attribute; it can be developed only through *learning*. But, as alluded
to earlier in the previous chapter, one cannot acquire any of the
essential managerial skills entirely from books, lectures, seminars, and
workshops;[22] many aspects of managerial competence are learnt best
in practice.

Let us now proceed to enhance our grasp of business communication by exploring the following: the nature of communication, the
communication process, communication effectiveness, internal communication, and external communication.

## 2.1 WHAT IS COMMUNICATION?

Essentially, the term "communication" is used to refer to the process
by which meaning and understanding are transacted between a given
*source* (a person, a group of persons, an organisation, or a government
agency) and a particular *receiver* (a person, a group of persons, an
organisation, or a government agency). As portrayed in Figure 2.1, it
implies an exchange or a sharing of meaning and understanding
between or among any given parties.

Good communication makes things happen in organisational settings; without it, work can stall because nobody can know what to do,
let alone the procedures to follow in executing work assignments. It

is through communication that any given organisational member can get to know about his or her responsibilities, authority, and accountabilities, as well as the various procedures, methods, and rules of the workplace. To any given organisation, therefore, *communication is, to an organisation, what the nervous system is to the human body*. This analogy should, optimistically, underscore the importance and critical nature of both efficient and effective communications in the success and survival of organisational entities.

Figure 2.1:  Communication as a Transaction

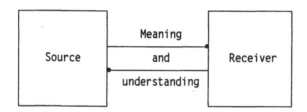

To illustrate the import and critical nature of communication, let us briefly consider its role in situations pertaining to each of the following important aspects of organisational life: decision making, job descriptions, performance standards, organisational objectives, introduction of change in organisational settings, accident prevention, and business negotiations.

1) DECISION MAKING.  In some organisations, especially public institutions, most important decisions (such as those pertaining to budget estimates, capital expenditures, hiring, pay levels, pay raises, promotions, demotions, transfers, dismissals, training, and the granting of loans to employees) are made through any one of the following two decision-making modes: "management by consensus," or "management by rules."[23] Decisions are made by "consensus" when they are arrived at by members of a formally constituted committee in a situation where there are no established guidelines or criteria to be followed in making decisions; they are made by "rules" when a committee or an

individual decision maker is expected to strictly adhere to laid down criteria or procedures in arriving at decisions.

Clearly, communication has a paramount role to play in each of the two decision-making modes described in the preceding paragraph. In using the first mode, for example, committee members need to deliberate freely and competently on any given issues or problems if they are to make sound, representative decisions concerning the problems or issues. In situations where the second mode applies, committee members or individual decision makers who are expected to make decisions need to be furnished with clearly and simply stated decision rules or criteria to facilitate easy comprehension and interpretation of the criteria or rules.

2) JOB DESCRIPTIONS. It is necessary for an employer to prepare job descriptions and clearly communicate them to organisational members if the organisational members are to perform their work effectively. It is perhaps axiomatic that, if members of an organisation are not apprised of what is required of them, the following, among other things, should be expected: non-performance of necessary tasks, possible duplication of effort, and role confusion.

3) PERFORMANCE STANDARDS. Standards of performance provide organisational members with guidelines for responsible action, which can lead to greater productivity. But unless these standards are communicated to employees in clear and specific terms, an organisation cannot expect its employees to attain desired results.

4) ORGANISATIONAL OBJECTIVES. Every organisation needs to formulate short-, intermediate-, and long-term objectives to serve as expectations against which to measure the results of organisational efforts. But such objectives are worthless if they are formulated but not emphatically communicated to organisational members who need them for direction.

5) INTRODUCTION OF CHANGE. Among the most important tasks performed in organisational settings is decision making. The outcomes of the decision-making process, that is, decisions, are about *changes* from an existing situation toward a desired state of being. But if an

organisation's structure does not provide for open, two-way communication among employees and work units, such changes can very likely nurture resentment, sabotage, and conflict. In other words, open, two-way communication can greatly minimise people's natural resistance to change by clearing any fears, doubts, and/or suspicions about the intentions and effects of any envisaged change programmes.

6) ACCIDENT PREVENTION. By and large, employees are trained to perform their work in efficient and effective ways by means of the following: *explaining* (verbal communication), *demonstrating* (non-verbal communication), and *reminding* (verbal communication). This approach of combining both verbal and non-verbal communication can also be applied in the prevention of accidents at places of work. A major requirement in this regard is for managers and/or supervisors to have the necessary knowledge and experience pertaining to safety, which they should be willing to unreservedly *share* with their underlings.

7) NEGOTIATIONS. Essentially, "negotiation" is the process by which two or more parties engage in discussions for the purpose of reaching a mutually satisfying business deal through an honest exchange of information. We all engage in negotiations of various forms wherever we happen to be at any particular time - at school, at work, during a job interview, at a garage, at an auto sales depot, or during collective bargaining. A major requirement in negotiations is for all the parties involved to develop a spirit of trust and understanding; it is perhaps not possible for any two or more parties to do an effective job of negotiating a business deal in an atmosphere that is void of mutual trust and understanding.

For all the good reasons, therefore, managers need to develop an aptitude to communicate effectively with peers, subordinates, superiors, external parties, and business associates. An indispensable requirement here is for them to foster open, two-way communication with all the parties they communicate with in different organisational or business situations - during interviews, in committees and other similar groupings and work units, and so forth. There should be no disputing the fact that an organisation's survival and level of produc-

tivity is directly dependent on how eloquently members of an organisation communicate amongst themselves and with parties outside
their organisation.

People who have worked in organisational settings for a long time
would probably testify to the fact that a communications problem or
breakdown in any given organisation can be just as perilous and
detrimental to the operations of the organisation as faulty or dysfunctional machinery and equipment. And, to digress somewhat, is it not
poor communication, and sometimes the lack thereof, that is often
cited as the fundamental cause of a great number of marriage breakdowns and other familial problems?

In passing, it is perhaps important to underscore the fact that
effectiveness in communicating with others is vital for people of all
walks of life; it is as important to Henry Kyambalesa, for example, as
it is to Nelson Mandela, Michael Jackson, Clint Eastwood, and Pope
John Paul the Second!

Before we proceed to discuss the communication process, let us
ask ourselves this question: why is it essential for managers to make
a determined effort to improve the efficiency and effectiveness of their
communication attempts? Of course it is because poor communication
can, as maintained earlier, lead to a misconception of a communicator's message and consequently hurt organisational performance.
Besides, poor communication on the part of the source of a communication attempt can raise a lot of questions about his or her aptitudes
and calibre. For example, what would one think about the calibre or
abilities of the communicator in the hypothetical situation presented
in Table 2.1 below?

TABLE 2.1: ERRORS IN MR STEVENSON'S PAPER

Recently, the business community in Stratford, Ontario, in Canada
initiated a programme intended to equip local business owners
with management and entrepreneurial skills through seminars,
workshops, and refresher courses. A couple of days ago, the
programme's organising committee unanimously agreed to launch
the first seminar within a fortnight, at which several speakers are

expected to give inaugural lectures. One of the invited speakers is Mr. Cox Stevenson, a former local-government official who now manages a chain of restaurants under the name "Surplus Foods Delicatessen." The following is an outline of the discussion paper entitled "Business Success in the 21st Century," which he has prepared for presentation at the seminar:

1/ **Succes Strategies**:
  1.1 Streamlining Oporations
  1.2 Being Inovative
  1.3 Seeking Lower Profit Magins
  1.4 Providing Credit Facilites

2/ **The Roll of Governments**

3/ **Summery and Conclusions**

4/ **The Changing Enviroment**:
  4.1 The Changing Consumar
  4.2 Harsh Economic Coditions
  4.3 Stiff Potencial Competition

5/ **Other Business Stratagies**:
  5.1 Beeing Customer-Orienteted
  5.2 Simprifying Product Designs
  5.3 Sourcing Cheeper In-puts

---

## 2.2 THE COMMUNICATION PROCESS

There are several basic elements which constitute the communication process; they are: (a) the *source* or origin of whatever is to be communicated, (b) the *channel* to be used in communicating the message, (c) the intended *receiver* of the message, and (d) the *feedback* loop to the origin of the message to convey or signal the effect or reaction evoked by the communication attempt. Figure 2.2 is a schematic representation of the communication process; it depicts each of the above-mentioned elements which characterise any given communication effort or attempt. Each of these elements is briefly described in the ensuing sections.

THE SOURCE

The source, origin, or sender is the individual, group of individuals, organisation, or government agency making the communication attempt. The source may have some idea, desired action, or meaning that is intended to be transmitted to another party. Whatever is intended for transmission will first be encoded or abstracted into symbols by the sender, and then organised into a message; how this is done may be described in a nutshell as follows: (a) *encoding*: the idea, thought, or desire to be communicated, which exists only in the mind of the source, has to be broken down and translated into symbols that have a high probability of conveying common meanings and understanding; and (b) the *message*: once the symbols are selected, they are arranged or organised into some sort of message that is to be transmitted through an appropriate channel to a designated receiver or audience.

Figure 2.2:  The Communication Process

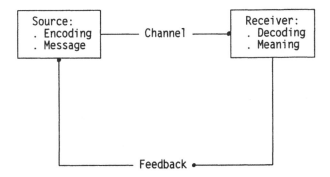

THE CHANNEL

The appropriate channel or medium by which the message is to be transmitted should now be selected. There are numerous channel choices open to communicators at any particular time for most communication attempts. Depending on the situation and the nature of the message, the communicator may choose to write a letter, write a memorandum, prepare a circular, place a notice on a bulletin board, transmit the message through a mailgram, transmit it by facsimile, use a telex machine, make a telephone call, broadcast the message through the radio or television, make gestures, or place the message in a regular publication (such as a newspaper, journal, directory, magazine, or catalogue).

1) BUSINESS LETTER. In business settings, letters (commonly written, typed, or printed on *letterheads*) are normally used as a vehicle for transmitting various kinds of messages to parties outside the organisation in which a particular communication attempt is initiated.

2) MEMORANDUM. A memorandum, which is commonly abbreviated to "memo," is an internal epistle; it is used as a channel or means for transmitting messages to individuals or work units within a given organisational entity.

3) CIRCULAR. The term "circular" is used here to refer to a leaflet or flyer prepared for dissemination to a designated audience. Generally, numerous copies are made of a given circular so that it can be distributed to a greater number of the people who constitute the communicator's target audience.

4) NOTICE. A "notice" is basically a short piece of writing designed to convey a message to a designated audience. Notices take various forms, such as the following: (a) posters or placards placed in public places stipulating the "dos and don'ts" in such places; (b) an announcement made through any given news media concerning a particular issue; and (c) a piece of writing placed on an organisation's bulletin board.

In preparing a notice, it is important to design an attractive format and select a set of conspicuous lettering; the level of success or failure of a notice to convey a message to the intended audience will partly be a direct result of its format and lettering. Other essential considerations in the preparation of notices should include the clarity of the message to be conveyed by the notice and the form the notice is to take to be able to reach the target audience successfully.

5) MAILGRAM. The origin of a communication effort may choose to electronically transmit a message to a post office nearest to the intended recipient of the message so that the post office can in turn transmit the message by mail to its destination. The piece of mail that may be dispatched by a given post office in this kind of arrangement is what is referred to here as a "mailgram."

6) TELEGRAM. A "telegram" is essentially a piece of mail containing a given sender's brief message transmitted by telegraph from one post office to another; the receiving post office sends the piece of mail to the addressee upon receipt of the telegraphically transmitted message.

7) FACSIMILE. By description, a "facsimile" is the process by which pictures and/or written messages are electronically transmitted (by means of a radio, telephone, or telegraph) and instantly reproduced at a distant place. The term is also used to refer to the reproduced pictures or messages.[24]

8) TELEX MACHINE. A "telex machine" is a piece of equipment used in making teletype communications through automatic exchanges. Telex machines work thus: as each letter and/or numeral of a message is typed onto the typewriter-like keyboard of the telex machine at the origin of a communication attempt, the telex machine at the receiving end automatically receives and prints the letter and/or numeral until the full message is transmitted and correspondingly printed out as a telex message. Sometimes, the "telex machine" is also referred to as a teleprinter, or a teletypewriter.

9) TELEPHONE. The "telephone" is an apparatus by which information is instantly transacted between the sender and the receiver through an exchange system owned and operated by a government-authorised organisation. Both the sender and the receiver use a similar type of equipment for orally transmitting and aurally receiving information.

10) RADIO AND TELEVISION. Business organisations also use the radio and/or television as communication channels, especially when the target audiences of their communications are such external parties as customers, suppliers, interest groups, local communities, and the like.

11) GESTURES. Essentially, gestures are a form of non-verbal communication; they are used either to supplement verbal communications or as a surrogate to verbal communications.

12) REGULAR PUBLICATIONS. Such regular publications as newspapers, journals, directories, magazines, and catalogues may also be used as communication channels for transmitting an organisation's messages on various matters and issues, more especially if such messages are intended for customers, suppliers, shareholders, or the general public.

## THE RECEIVER

The receiver is the person, group of persons, organisation, or society that the source (or sender) intends to communicate with. Two important roles are expected to be played by the receiver or receivers of any given message; these are, first, to decode the message received and, second, to attach some meaning to the message. These two roles are briefly described immediately below.

1) *Decoding.* Upon receiving the transmitted message, the receiver has the task of decoding or interpreting it in order to abstract some meaning from it. How correctly or incorrectly the receiver interprets any communications received depends largely on such factors as the following: level of education, familiarity with the subject matter of the message, perception, personality, mental and physical health, environmental conditions, and so forth. Most of these factors are cited and discussed as common communication barriers elsewhere in this chapter.

2) *Meaning.* After interpreting the message, the receiver then attaches a meaning to it. As explained in the ensuing section, a communication effort can be said to be successful only when the intended receiver or audience interprets the message involved as contemplated by the origin.

## FEEDBACK

This is the means by which the receiver changes roles and becomes the source; that is, the receiver attempts to communicate back to the source of a given message by means of the feedback loop in the communication process. With the successful completion of each step in the communication process, the meaning abstracted from the message by the receiver should be the same as that intended by the sender. If this occurred, we would say that the communication was effective or successful, meaning, in other words, that the intended receiver or audience received the message and attached to it the meaning similar to that intended by the source.

It should be emphasised, however, that it is quite another thing to say that the communication effort or attempt was *efficient*. In communication, "efficiency" means making a communication attempt with the least possible "cost." The cost alluded to here may include such elements as effort expended, money spent, or comfort foregone. A communication attempt is relatively efficient, for example, if the message is transmitted through a channel at less cost to the source than that required by alternative channels.

It is usually necessary for communicators to make a trade-off between communication efficiency and effectiveness. A communication attempt, for example, may be highly efficient (that is, least costly), yet the intended receiver or target audience may never receive the message transmitted, or the meaning inferred may be completely different from the meaning intended by the origin of the communication attempt. Take the example of a college professor who wishes to communicate his decision to re-schedule a regularly scheduled lecture supposed to be delivered to a class of fifty-five students the following day to the day after. He may consider several alternatives, such as the following:

1) Prepare a circular addressed to the class and indiscriminately post a copy under every door to each room in students' halls of residence;

2) Prepare a memorandum addressed to the class and send a photo copy to each of the fifty-five students through the campus mail system;

3) Prepare a notice and place several copies of it on bulletin boards within the institution's premises; or

4) Find out the other classes which each of the fifty-five students takes and send a secretary to notify them individually about the re-scheduled lecture.

Clearly, these four alternatives differ in terms of *efficiency* (cost) and *effectiveness* (accomplishment). For example, while the first alternative is the most effective, it is the most inefficient among the four alternatives. Similarly, while the last alternative is the least effective, it is apparently the most efficient. Therefore, communicators should always try to make a trade-off between communication efficiency and effectiveness, taking into account the nature and importance of what is to be communicated; the following hints are important in this endeavour:

1) In making communications pertaining to new organisational policies, procedures, and programmes which are pertinent to the smooth running of an organisation and its constituent units, effectiveness should override efficiency;

2) External or organisation-based communications which have neither direct nor indirect effects on the operations of an organisation should be undertaken with greater concern for efficiency than for effectiveness; and

3) Routine communications merely intended to remind employees and other parties about existing organisational programmes, policies, and procedures should be made with equal concern for both efficiency and effectiveness.

## 2.3 COMMUNICATION EFFECTIVENESS

As stated earlier, "effective" communication means that the intended receiver or audience receives and correctly interprets the sender's message. This, however, does not always happen due to communication barriers. There are numerous individual-based, environmental, and situational factors which play an important role in the interpretations people give to the various kinds of messages they receive; sometimes, these stimuli are so strong that they are interpreted instead of the messages communicated. When these factors or stimuli sway the communication receiver's understanding to a degree that does not harmonise well with the meaning intended by the communicator, they become "barriers" to the clear interpretation of information or messages received. This section is intended to survey the *common barriers* to effective communication, as well as important *facilitators* to communication.

THE COMMON BARRIERS

Among the common barriers to effective communication that organisational members should be aware of are the following: differences in perception among people; lack of the necessary knowledge about what to communicate, or what is communicated; the mental and physical health of any of the parties involved in a communication effort; the psychological or emotional conditions of either the sender or the receiver; personality differences among people communicating with each other; biases or prejudices among people engaged in communications; physical distractions like noise and poor illumination; poor organisation of ideas by the sender; poor listening; excessive information, or communication overload; speech problems like stammering and perverted speech resulting from inebriation; slurred utterance or pronunciation; and such grammar-related barriers as semantic, syntactic, and/or orthographic errors in transmitted messages. A brief description of each of these common barriers to the success of communication efforts follows in the ensuing paragraphs.

1) PERCEPTION. The term "perception" is used here to refer to the different ways in which people organise and interpret the various kinds of stimuli they receive, such as information. Every person has a somewhat different way of interpreting things they see, read, or hear - an aspect about people which, to a certain degree, affects the success and effectiveness of communication efforts in which they may be involved.

2) LIMITED KNOWLEDGE. An individual's prior grasp of the subject about which he or she is to write or converse can greatly enable him

or her to do an effective job of exploring the subject. Similarly, communication receivers can more successfully interpret the communications they receive if they are thoroughly conversant with the subject matter of such communications. Unfortunately, though, communication senders and receivers often engage in communications pertaining to subjects on which they have no sufficient knowledge. In general, therefore, limited knowledge among people tends to play a part in many communication failures and misconstructions.

3) PERSON'S CONDITION. There are many individual-based factors which can very easily thwart the success and effectiveness of communications in business settings; the more important of these factors include the mental, emotional, psychological, and physical state of a given individual. A person who is mentally deranged, for example, cannot possibly engage in a meaningful dialogue with other members of society.

4) PERSONALITY. The term "personality" refers to a person's consistent pattern of behaviour. Sometimes, a person's personality can mitigate the effectiveness of communications; in a discussion, for example, a person who has a domineering personality is likely to talk more and listen less, thus preventing other parties from making their full contribution to the discussion. Also, if a person is an introvert, he or she is likely to interact and converse with others in a reserved manner, consequently limiting the flow of information or ideas.

5) BIASES. There is perhaps not a single person in the entire world who does not harbour certain unfair and/or unfounded opinions about other people. These opinions, which an individual may hold either consciously or otherwise, can very easily affect the individual's interpretation of information or messages received from people about whom they are prejudiced in a particular way.

6) DISTRACTIONS. There is a multiplicity of distractions in organisational settings which can frustrate an individual's attempt to transmit or receive important messages. Examples of such distractions include the following: (a) the din of machinery and equipment, which can impede telephone and interpersonal communications; (b) poor illumination,

which can have an adverse effect on people's ability to peruse written communications; and (c) the additional activities in which a person may be involved while receiving or transmitting messages.

7) MUDDLED IDEAS. Whether they are to be presented orally or in writing, ideas need to be organised in a coherent manner if they are to be construed with little or no difficulty. But all too often, some people ignore this requirement; they organise and present their ideas haphazardly, hence making it hard for their target audiences to discern the gist of the ideas.

8) POOR LISTENING. It is often hard to come across a good listener. Most of the people I have come across, for example, have a tendency to try to assume a dominant role in discussions; they seem to delight in talking more and listening less, so to speak. This propensity for people to dominate discussions seem to emanate from the following, among other things: (a) a conscious desire to display one's knowledge; (b) a feeling of being more important than the other party, which motivates a person to try to dominate a discussion in a bid to relegate the other party to a passive and inferior position; and (c) a deliberate effort to ensure that discussions are restricted to subjects with which one is familiar.

Inadequate listening is a generally more salient communication problem when one is involved in an argument with a person whose views are radically different from one's own. In such a situation, it is not unusual for a person to overly concentrate on pondering a defence while the rival is expounding his or her viewpoint. This unfortunate tendency among people who are involved in an encounter that is somewhat in the nature of polemics usually leads to failure in discerning the basis or rationality of each other's points of view.

9) COMMUNICATION OVERLOAD. Some communicators stuff their target receivers with a surfeit of information and give them unrealistic time limits within which they are to take action based on such information. This can, no doubt, affect the communication receivers' ability to adequately analyse and productively utilise the information received.

10) IMPAIRED SPEECH. Certain people have speech difficulties emanat-

ing from dysfunctional vocal cords, while others may be troubled by stammering or distorted speech culminating from inebriation. These and any other similar forms of speech impairment can be a very serious hurdle in oral communications.

11) SLURRED SPEECH. There are some individuals who find it fashionable to pronounce words indistinctively,[25] or to speak in a hurried manner. Unfortunately, this can very easily lead to failure by the intended receiver or receivers to comprehend the message communicated.

12) GRAMMATICAL PROBLEMS. In general, grammar-related barriers permeate all communications made in business settings, more especially when communication senders and/or receivers are not sufficiently proficient in the language of communication - such as in situations where the language used is not the mother tongue of the parties involved. Specifically, grammar-related communication barriers can occur in any of the following forms: (a) *semantic barriers*: these are barriers occasioned by the communicator's use of words whose meanings are not conventionally in consonance with the issue or situation being addressed; (b) *syntactic barriers*: these emanate from improper sentence construction by the communicator, which can pose problems for the intended communication receiver or receivers in discerning the gist of a message received; and (c) *orthographic barriers*: these are communication barriers which are caused by incorrect or non-standard spellings in written communications.

OVERCOMING THE BARRIERS

There are many different ways in which the origin of a communication attempt and the intended receiver or receivers can positively contribute to communication effectiveness;[26] these different ways or "facilitators" are cited and discussed in a nutshell in the three sections that follow immediately below.

1) THE SENDER. Communicators can increase the effectiveness of their communications in many ways, including the following: properly timing their communications, organising the ideas they wish to communi-

cate, placing a premium on brevity, communicating in moderation, and making a good choice of words to be used. Each of these communication facilitators is briefly discussed in the ensuing paragraphs.

a) *Proper Timing*: Timing one's communications can greatly contribute to the success and effectiveness of one's communication efforts. If a communicator cannot consider the appropriateness of a given situation or period of time before he or she makes a communication attempt, there is a likelihood that such a communication attempt will be unsuccessful. The following are examples of poor timing which communicators should avoid: (i) attempting to communicate an important message to someone amid deafening noises at a sporting game or along a busy highway; (ii) communicating more than the intended receiver or audience can intelligibly decipher within a given period of time, like a teacher who gives his students a fifty-page handout as preparatory material for a test to be administered thirty minutes later; (iii) making an important telephone call against the din of falling hailstones; (iv) communicating work-related details to a grieving person.

b) *Well-Organised Ideas*: Communicators need to organise their ideas systematically to make it easy for intended receivers to understand them. An important requirement in getting one's ideas coherently organised is the grouping and presentation of one's ideas according to their nature; for example, a discourse on the pros and cons of a particular organisational policy should exhaustively explore all the "pros" before turning to the "cons" of the policy, or vice versa, rather than explore them in a jumbled manner. Also, a report on the occurrence of an event should be prepared in a chronological fashion to make it more conceivable to the intended receiver or audience.

c) *Brevity*: Some communications require people who transmit them to deliberately try to be men or women of "few words." Such communications include those pertaining to job instructions, work assignments, and operating procedures; these and other similar categories of organisational communications need to be brief and to the point if the people for whom they are intended are to vividly apprehend them for subsequent use in attaining desired end results.

d) *Moderation*: Communication attempts, like many other efforts made in day-to-day organisational life, need to be made in moderation. The audience or audiences of any communication attempt have a limit to which they can effectively handle the amount of information which they may receive at any particular time. It is, therefore, incumbent upon communicators to guard against overloading their intended audiences with excessive information in order to improve the effectiveness of their communication efforts.

e) *Clarity and Conciseness*: The sender's ability to communicate clearly and concisely both orally and in writing can greatly contribute to the success and effectiveness of any communication attempt. It should perhaps be common knowledge that inaccurate, muddled, and/or ambiguous communications, regardless of whether they are transmitted orally or in writing, can tarnish the image and reputation of both the communicator and his or her organisation. This should be a good reason why communicators need to develop a rich business vocabulary to be able to express themselves clearly and accurately in all their business communications, such as when they write formal letters, prepare memoranda or reports, engage in deliberations during meetings or interviews, or engage in interpersonal communications with other professional folk. With respect to the writing of formal letters, managers would perhaps do well to embrace Kilpatrick's admonition:

> *A poorly spelled letter is a gravy-stained tie ...*
> *[w]hen in doubt about the spelling of a word, look it*
> *up! And stay in doubt!*[27]

f) *Word Choice*: The choice of appropriate words and phrases (that is, words and phrases which have a high probability of matching the educational or professional level of a particular communication receiver or audience) is an essential consideration for people whose communications have a bearing on the functioning and operations of an organisation or any of its constituent units. By and large, communicators can succeed in selecting words or phrases which their audiences can easily comprehend or accurately interpret if they are empathetic, that is, if they are capable of understanding the receiver's personality, level of education, and, among other things, professional characteristics.

2) THE RECEIVER. The intended receivers in any given communication process can greatly contribute to the success and effectiveness of communication efforts. They can achieve this in many different ways, including the following: taking notes, active involvement, and seeking clarification. A brief discussion of each of these efforts follows.

a) *Taking Notes*: People who make an effort to take down notes as they receive communications by telephone, at a seminar, or in their bosses' offices greatly facilitate the success of communications. The notes are useful in the following ways, among others: (i) they can later serve as a reminder to the receiver about the communication; and (ii) they can save the receiver from the trouble or inconvenience of having to commit the specifics of the message or information received to memory.

b) *Active Involvement*: In receiving information or messages, communication receivers should, of necessity, develop veritable interest in such communications, as well as get actively involved in the process; in all probability, communication senders will be stimulated to execute their communication efforts more enthusiastically when their target receivers adopt a receptive and sprightly posture.

c) *Seeking Clarification*: Communication receivers can greatly contribute to the efficacy of communication efforts if they develop a habit of seeking clarification on communications (or any part thereof) about which they may have doubts or queries. Some people are bashful about seeking clarification on messages or instructions whose content or objective they may be uncertain about and, thereof, try to respond or take action on the basis of what they personally guess or suppose to be the purpose or content of the instructions or messages received. Unfortunately, actions or responses based on guesses or suppositions of what the messages or instructions received are intended to accomplish can very easily turn out to be incongruent with those anticipated by the origin of the messages or instructions.

3) SENDER AND RECEIVER. As portrayed earlier in Figure 2.1, communication essentially involves exchanges of common meanings and understanding between the origin and the intended target or targets of a given communication effort. For any such exchanges to be accomplished effectively, the following communication facilitators are perhaps indispensable: empathy, two-way communication, objectivity, emotional control, wide knowledge, minimum distractions, allowance for error, and being practical.

a) *Empathy*: There is a need for both communication initiators and receivers to develop the ability to put themselves in other people's shoes and understand the biases, interests, and communication abilities of all the parties they communicate with. Unless they are empathetic, initiators and intended audiences of communications can thwart the success of communication efforts. It should be common knowledge, for example, that the choice of appropriate words and phrases which are likely to be more comprehensible to the parties an individual is to communicate with is possible only when one is empathetic.

b) *Two-Way Exchange*: Communication, as maintained earlier in this chapter, is essentially a process involving the "transaction" or sharing of meanings and understanding between any two or more parties. Clearly, this requires parties involved in communications to be committed to fostering free, two-way communication flows. In conversations, for example, a smooth, two-way exchange of information can be fostered and facilitated through such efforts as the following: (i) listening advertently and receptively when it is the other party's turn to talk; (ii) avoiding the common temptation of being a bit too defensive of one's views or opinions about the subject at hand; (iii) guarding against listening for negative or positive words because this can lead to out-of-context interpretation of any words which may be taken from whatever is said by the other party; and (iv) stimulating the other party to talk further with nods and such props as "Really?" and "Gee!"

In discussions or conversations that take the form of an argument, the basic solution to the problem of inadequate listening (which was described earlier in this chapter in the section on "poor listening") is for each party involved in the argument to seek to reach a balance between listening and talking or thinking up one's response. Also important in this regard is the need to accept defeat when it comes and, by so doing, avoid arguing just for the sake of it. In general, a simple recipe for good listening is the following joke:

> The fact that we have two ears and one mouth implies
> that we are supposed to listen twice as much as we
> are supposed to talk.

c) *Objectivity*: A person's subjective judgment or classification of other people, which may be based on a particular criterion or characteristic, can affect the nature of his or her communications with such people. For example, a man who fetishes wealth may tend to evaluate people on the basis of their material possessions and may, as a result, be more inclined to exert more effort on effectuating his communications with well-to-do people and less effort, if any at all, on improving his communications with paupers. In other words, the relevance or importance of the communications will be subjectively determined on the basis of how wealthy the person he is communicating with is. Such forms of subjectivity need to be wrestled if a person ever wishes to improve his or her communications in business settings.

A related problem here concerns our subjective, culturally derived perception of phenomena in the world around us, which generally sets the stage for the manner in which we interpret and/or present information in business settings. An important step in overcoming this problem is perhaps the recognition of the fact that our views and perceptions will seldom be shared by the people with whom we communicate in our day-to-day business pursuits and endeavours. In general, it is good practice not to allow our subjective or parochial views and perceptions to supersede objective, polished, and eclectic reasoning.

d) *Emotional Control*: The emotional state of a person involved in communications is an important element in his or her ability to communicate effectively; it is perhaps not humanly possible for a person who is emotionally laden to communicate rationally and objectively with other people. Therefore, it is necessary for all parties who may happen to be involved in important communications to control their emotions, or, alternatively, to avoid engaging in communications during times when they are emotionally charged. For people who stammer, the need for emotional control is perhaps even more critical as they are likely to find it more difficult to articulate when they are in an emotional state.

e) *Wide Knowledge*: In concluding the preface to this book, I presented the following excerpt from Proverbs 3, verses 13 and 14: "Happy is the man that findeth wisdom and the man that getteth understanding, for the merchandise of it is better than the merchandise of silver, and the gain thereof than fine gold." How many people would disagree with the message conveyed by this adage? Is it not knowledge (and its wise application) which saves us from being at the behest of the ever-increasing turbulence in our social, economic, and business milieus? The bottom line for those of us who fare in the modern business arena is to gain adequate knowledge of the novelties of the world around us, in spite of the limitations posed by the "information explosion" that is characteristic of our era, which we have to learn to live with because, like the weather, it has certainly come to stay.

To put it more succinctly, business and organisational life requires us to have wide and intimate knowledge of a broad spectrum of issues and aspects relating to the environment in which business activities are undertaken and, perhaps more importantly, the esoteric language and terminology of our specific professions; only when we meet this requirement can we be able to engage productively in business communications and facilitate the attainment of both organisational and personal goals. The acquisition of extensive knowledge can be accomplished in a number of ways, including the following: (i) attending seminars, workshops, and refresher courses on a regular basis; (ii) reading widely; and (iii) engaging in professional discussions during social outings and get-togethers.

f) *Minimum Distractions*: Communication attempts cannot possibly be successfully consummated in a setting that is fraught with physical or other kinds of distractions. For this reason, communicators and their intended audiences need to identify and minimise or remove any distractions that are likely to mitigate the effectiveness of communication efforts in which they are involved. Sometimes, important formal activities can also become distractions to each other if a communicator attempts to perform them all at once; for example, a foreman is not likely to perform the following tasks effectively if he attempts to perform them simultaneously: (i) delegating a set of assignments to an underling over the telephone; (ii) totalling up the costs of production inputs on an adding machine; and (iii) dictating to his secretary about a fire which occurred in the production plant the previous night. Communicators should, therefore, guard against the temptation of engaging in more communication efforts than they can effectively handle at any particular time.

g) *Allowance for Error*: It is important for both the sender and the receiver of communications to expect and tolerate human error at any step of the communication process. After all, even the most eloquent speakers and prolific writers cannot claim to be flawless in their works; perhaps the following maxims will somewhat make the point more clearly:

> *Whoever thinks a faultless piece to see thinks what never was, nor is, nor ever shall be.*[28] And

> *To err is human.*[29]

Excessive concern for perfection in organisational communications should, therefore, be avoided because it is unrealistic and, moreover, has the unfortunate potential to detract communicators and/or their target audiences from performing the tasks the communications may be intended to facilitate. However, communicators should guard against using this allowance for human error to justify mediocre communication attempts emanating from carelessness, poor grammar, and the like. Communication receivers, on the other hand, should avoid developing a fault-finding or perfectionist attitude.

h) *Being Practical*: Parties involved in any given communication effort need to avoid being pedantic; also, they should be wary of nit-picking. In other words, the primary concern in business communications should be substance; frivolity, pedantry, and superfluity should never be permitted to overshadow the essence of any given communication effort.

## 2.4 INTERNAL COMMUNICATION

The term "internal communication" refers to any and all kinds of messages transmitted and received within a given organisation. Such communication may either be formal or informal. It is said to be "formal" when the information or messages are transmitted through a structure that is formally developed by an organisation's corporate management. Examples of such communications include the following: business reports, company news bulletins, and communications which take place during committee meetings and interviews. Internal communication is said to be "informal" when it is accomplished through channels that are not officially established by the corporate management of the organisation involved.

### FORMAL COMMUNICATION

The manner in which formal organisations are structured provides for the transmission of important messages in three directions as follows: from superiors down to subordinates, from subordinates up the organisation to superiors, and from one individual or group of individuals to another at the same level of authority in the organisation. In more precise terms, the formal internal communications of any given organisation take the following three forms: downward communication, upward communication, and horizontal communication.[30] A detailed description of each of these three important forms of formal organisational communication follows in the ensuing sections.

1) DOWNWARD COMMUNICATION. Organisation-based communications which are generally designated as "downward communication" are those initiated by organisational members in higher echelons of an

organisation; they are intended for individuals and work units at lower levels of an organisation. The forms which such communications take include the following: job instructions, explanations pertaining to the rationale of jobs or positions, policy stipulations, details on work procedures, feedback on employees' performance, indoctrination communications, details on conditions of service, and stipulations of important organisational rules and regulations. Each of these forms of organisational communications is described in a nutshell below.

a) *Job Instructions*: These are aimed at explaining how an organisational member is expected to perform a given task, the different types of materials and machinery and equipment to be used, and, in certain instances, the kinds of clothing he or she may be required to put on while performing the designated task.

b) *Job Rationale*: This is essentially a set of statements intended to inform employees about how their different jobs or positions relate to the other jobs or positions in their organisations, as well as the importance of their jobs or positions in the attainment of departmental and, eventually, overall organisational goals.

c) *Policies*: An organisation's policies are general decision guidelines and rules of thumb designed to guide the behaviour, decisions, and operations of work units, managerial personnel, supervisory personnel, and the workers in lower levels of an organisation; they reflect the beliefs and business philosophy of top management folk who generate and promulgate them.

d) *Work Procedures*: Basically, procedures outline the sequence in which a task or activity is expected or supposed to be performed or accomplished, and indicate the individuals and/or work units responsible at each phase of the sequence; they are designed to serve as a safeguard against pell-mell execution of an organisation's plans and/or day-to-day work activities.

e) *Feedback on Performance*: This generally includes all the various kinds of information intended to apprise employees of how well or badly their performance is rated by their immediate supervisors.

Balanced performance appraisals - that is, those which clearly point out both satisfactory and unsatisfactory performance on the job - can greatly help employees in determining the kinds of work behaviour they need to sustain and those they need to dispense with in order to improve their ratings in future performance appraisals.

f) *Indoctrination Communications*: The downward communications which generally fall under this classification include those which are aimed at influencing employees to conform to the dictates of their organisation and develop positive attitudes toward its policies, goals, and *modus operandi*.

g) *Working Conditions*: Communications pertaining to employees' working conditions provide organisational members with the necessary details on such aspects as pay levels, career ladder (sometimes referred to as "career progression"), fringe benefits, terminal benefits, and the like.

h) *Disciplinary Code*: Every organisation provides a set of rules and regulations which stipulate acceptable and unacceptable behaviour at work, as well as disciplinary actions which may be taken against employees who may not comply with any of the stipulated rules and regulations. Disciplinary codes usually include time, insubordination, safety, and prohibited-behaviour rules and regulations.

By and large, the purpose of downward communication is to increase employees' understanding of their organisations, as well as their jobs. Various means are used by organisations to communicate downward, such as the following: face-to-face verbal interaction, written instructions, and company manuals, magazines, and bulletin boards.

2) UPWARD COMMUNICATION. Communications flowing upwards in an organisation originate from work units or individuals in the lower ranks of the organisation; they are intended for organisational members at higher hierarchical levels. These communications may generally consist of such types of information as those pertaining to performance levels, complaints and grievances, suggestions, financial

statements, budgets, and attrition.

a) *Performance Levels*: Information pertaining to the performance levels of an organisation's work units and individual employees provides a basis for making the appropriate operational decisions that are needed to improve operational efficiency and effectiveness. Without such information, an organisation's top management has basically no basis for making critical operational decisions and cannot, therefore, wield enough leverage to steer the organisation to success.

b) *Complaints and Grievances*: In organisational settings, employees often encounter a myriad of personal and work-related problems. Some of these problems are less serious and can be attended to by affected employees' immediate supervisors; such problems are generally and conveniently designated as "complaints." Other problems facing employees are those which are more serious and which, as such, require the involvement and preponderance of higher management folk to resolve; these are generally referred to as "grievances."

c) *Suggestions*: Innovative organisations find it necessary to provide for a suggestion system and encourage organisational members to freely contribute ideas and make suggestions intended to increase output, improve the quality of products, reduce on-the-job accidents, improve operational efficiency, and/or change counter-productive and undesirable policies and practices. As a general practice, employees are advised to submit their ideas or make their suggestions (either in person or anonymously) to someone in top management rather than to their immediate supervisors; this is done to prevent any possible suppression of employees' innovative ideas and suggestions by their immediate supervisors.

d) *Financial Statements*: An organisation's financial statements, which include the balance sheet and the income statement, are prepared by accounting personnel for top management. They contain very valuable information which top management can use in making important corporate and operational decisions that will facilitate the attainment of desired levels of organisational performance and profitability.

e) *Budgets*: The term "budget" is used here to refer to any projection of revenues and expenditures prepared by an operating unit to serve as a tool for controlling the activities and operations of the operating unit and its constituent members (that is, managers, supervisors, and operatives). Normally, budgets are prepared and submitted to top management by operating units for sanctioning before they can be used formally as control tools. Entire organisational entities also prepare budgets, which, essentially, are revenue and expenditure projections reflecting the aggregates of the projected revenues and expenditures of constituent operating units.

f) *Attrition*: The term "attrition" is applied here to refer to the gradual reduction of an organisation's work force caused by a regular exit of organisational members who, for various reasons, decide to voluntarily terminate their employment in the organisation. Since management is expected to maintain an optimal number of personnel to perform organisational tasks at any given time, some organisations make it mandatory for heads of units to regularly furnish management with, *inter alia*, details pertaining to employee attrition in their sections or departments to enable it to make sound personnel-related decisions, such as those concerning the following aspects of conditions of service: (i) personnel or employee acquirement; (ii) salaries, wages, and fringe benefits; (iii) hours of work; (iv) promotions; and (v) training opportunities.

These and any other forms of upward communications are important because they are the major means by which organisational members at higher echelons of an organisation get a feel of what is going on at lower levels where production and other pertinent operations and activities are undertaken. Without such communications, there is probably no way decision makers can gauge the necessary information for making decisions that will lead to greater and optimal levels of organisational efficiency and effectiveness.

3) HORIZONTAL COMMUNICATION. In organisational settings, "horizontal communication" takes place between and among individual employees or work units that are at the same level of authority. There are several major ways in which horizontal communications are used in organisat-

ions; they include: (a) coordination of the tasks and activities of individual employees and work units; (b) solving technical, human relations, and other problems that emanate from interactions between and among individual employees and/or work units as they discharge or perform their duties; (c) sharing of information that is pertinent to the operations and other aspects of an organisation; and (d) resolution of conflicts between and among individual employees and/or work units.

### INFORMAL COMMUNICATION

The forms of organisational communications which are designated as "informal communication" are those which take place through channels that are not created or prescribed by management. Such communications take place through what is generally referred to as the "grapevine." Generally, the grapevine is much faster at transmitting information than formal communication channels. This aspect often poses a problem to managers and supervisors when it comes to dealing with information that is of great interest to organisational members and which is likely to be distorted or misinterpreted if it were transmitted through the informal communication network.

1) NATURE OF THE GRAPEVINE. The term "grapevine" is used in the management lingo to refer to the informal channel of communication by which confidential information that is important to employees is transmitted, usually from higher to lower echelons of an organisation. Informal communication networks develop spontaneously to facilitate the unofficial circulation of classified information that is under the aegis of management to meet organisational members' information needs which cannot be met through formal communication channels due to confidentiality, corporate policy, and/or other reasons. As such, informal channels of communication are probably more potent and well-developed in organisations where top management has a posture that is characterised by dreadful secrecy, formality, and confidentiality. In such organisations, it would not be generally uncommon to find a ghastly aura of mistrust, suspicion, scepticism, and antagonism among organisational members.

There are several organisational issues and matters about which members of an organisation strive to be apprised of through the grape-vine, and which make the grapevine a particularly important source of vital information for organisational members who are deprived of information on these matters and issues; they include the following: compensation issues, promotions, disciplinary matters, threatening situations, and envisaged organisational changes. These aspects, which are briefly discussed in the remainder of this section, also tend to incite "liaison" persons to seek the necessary confidential information which they can pass over to expectant organisational members.

a) *Compensation Matters*: Information on issues concerning wages, salaries, fringe benefits, and other forms of extrinsic rewards is of great interest to employees and is, therefore, among the various kinds of information regularly shared by organisational members through the grapevine. In unionised organisations, for example, workers tend to be informally well-apprised of the necessary details about deliberations and resolutions on compensation matters during the course of any union-management negotiations which may be held to consider such matters.

b) *Promotions*: Management decisions concerning the appointment of deserving organisational members to higher positions usually get into the "ear" of the grapevine soon after they are made and long before they are officially promulgated by the management people who make them.

c) *Disciplinary Matters*: By and large, decisions made by manage-ment pertaining to the nature and severity of disciplinary actions to be taken against erring organisational members get known quickly throughout an organisation by unofficial means before they are formally divulged. Depending on the seriousness of the breach involved, the disciplinary actions which an organisation's management may find appropriate may take any of the following forms: warning, lateral transfer, suspension with or without pay, demotion, or summary dismissal.

d) *Threatening Situations*: When organisational members are facing a threatening situation (such as a management-envisaged cutback in the work force, layoffs, a plant closure, and the like), they cannot possibly rest until they gain advance information regarding, among other things, the security of their jobs; and since management will usually try to "put a lid" on details and decisions pertaining to such situations until the time is right to carry out contemplated plans, organisational members will actively seek to obtain the information they need much in advance by informal means.

e) *Organisational Changes*: Planned organisational changes (such as those concerning major re-organisation of organisational units, policy changes, change in the ownership of an organisation, and so forth) can arouse employees to informally seek out details on anticipated effects and other important aspects of the changes which are not officially explained to them by top management.

2) PROS AND CONS OF THE GRAPEVINE. The grapevine is a benign component of organisational life; it has certain important advantages, such as the following: it enhances job satisfaction, supplements an organisation's formal channels of communication, and facilitates social interactions among organisational members. Each of these functions is described in a nutshell below.

a) *Enhancing Job Satisfaction*: Informal communication channels can have positive effects on job satisfaction among members of an organisation. This is possible in the following ways, among others: (a) employees' informal access to confidential information reduces the anxiety that is often associated with not having any knowledge about top management's short-, intermediate-, and long-term plans and policies which are likely to have unfavourable effects on their welfare; and (b) employees who obtain confidential information and convey it to other organisational members find their role very fulfilling, especially that they are expressly or otherwise regarded by others as important sources of classified information. In these and other ways, therefore, the grapevine can, to a certain degree, elevate job satisfaction in organisational settings.

b) *Supplementing Formal Channels*: There are certain things in organisations which cannot be attained entirely through formal communications. For example, orientation of new employees cannot possibly be accomplished entirely through formally organised orientation programmes; informal communications between new and veteran employees also play an important role in the orientation process. In fact, experience has taught us that new employees in any given organisation learn more about their new work environment from informal communications and interactions with old employees than they do from official orientation programmes.

c) *Facilitating Social Interactions*: The grapevine can provide the means by which organisational members can meet or satisfy their social needs at work. Among the important social needs which can be met through the grapevine include the *need for belonging* and the *need for affiliation*, both of which are important to employees. Essentially, the grapevine facilitates the socialisation process when and as individuals seek out confidential information which is vital to them.

*Disadvantages*. The grapevine, however, is not without disadvantages; its unofficial presence in organisational settings is usually viewed as being detrimental to organisational well-being because of its potential to breed conflict and undermine confidentiality. The rumour-mongering which the grapevine facilitates can very easily create tension and conflict between an organisation's decision makers and its rank and file. No doubt, such a situation can have adverse effects on the operations of an organisation. And, in terms of its potential to violate or undermine an organisation's necessary confidentiality, the grapevine is a potent channel of communication which can very likely unveil information that is classified by an organisation's management to prevent it from filtering out to competitors, who may need such occult information for use in their efforts to frustrate the organisation's business pursuits and endeavours.

3) LIVING WITH THE GRAPEVINE. In spite of its potential onerous effects on the success of an organisation, the grapevine is a natural component of organisational life which cannot be averted, banished, or wished away; it is an indelible element of organisational life which the management in any and every organisation can only do well to accommodate and use to the best advantage of the organisation. To

accomplish this, management needs to remove the communication "valves" which unnecessarily give managers, administrators, and supervisors a monopoly on information that is important to the bulk of organisational members and, by so doing, facilitate and expedite the flow of information through both the grapevine and the formal communication channels.

In other words, it is essential for management to create an organisational culture in which there is open, two-way communication among organisational members to mitigate rumour-mongering, as well as the possible distortion of important information that is likely to find its way into the alert and sprightly "ear" of the grapevine.

## 2.5 EXTERNAL COMMUNICATION

In addition to their involvement in various forms of internal communications, managers also engage in very extensive communications with each of the various segments of their organisations' publics in society, including national governments, municipal authorities, chambers of commerce and industry, customers, suppliers, financial institutions, shareholders, and the like. Communication exchanges between managers and each of these parties is what constitutes "external" communication.

A great deal of any given organisation's external communications, whether they are with parties in its domestic or foreign environments, are accomplished through the following functions: marketing communication, and public relations.[31] A survey of the marketing communication effort follows; the other function, that is, public relations, is discussed later in Chapter 4.

### MARKETING COMMUNICATION

The term "marketing communication" refers to the process or means by which sales-promoting information and/or messages are schemed and eventually transmitted from an organisation to its various customer groups. The transmission of marketing information or messages is accomplished through several sales-getting efforts and is facilitated by the marketing communication process; these promotional efforts and the facilitating process are the themes of discussion in this section.

1) SALES-GETTING EFFORTS. An organisation's communications pertaining to the promotion of its products includes the following sales-getting tools or efforts, which are among the many elements of what is generally referred to as the *promotional mix*: advertising, publicity, sales talk, impulsive mail, emissary-style promotion, and customer relations. A brief description of each of these six sales-getting tools follows.

a) *Advertising*: Essentially, "advertising" is a sponsored form of promotional communication that is transmitted through the mass media. Among the common media that are often used are journals, newspapers, the Internet, magazines, rented roadside benches, signboards, directories, catalogues, rented billboards, television, and the radio. On radio and television, common forms of advertising are single-shot commercials, "infomercials", and event sponsorship. Institu-tions, as well as individuals, use advertising to promote such things as goods, services, ideas, programmes of study, and political candidates. Canadian economist Stephen Leacock, though, has described advertising more simplistically (although provocatively, perhaps, from the standpoint of consumers) as "the art of arresting human intelligence long enough to get money from it."[32]

b) *Publicity*: The term "publicity" is broadly used here to refer to the following promotional efforts: (i) self-erected billboards along major streets and highways; (ii) point-of-sale posters; (iii) placards near an organisation's business premises; (iv) writings on product packages, shirts, caps, vehicles, walls of buildings, and so on; (v) self-improvised roadside benches; (vi) provision of informative desk and/or wall calendars to prospective buyers; and (vii) positive information (not sponsored by the organisation) transmitted by news reporters, consumer associations, and other parties about the organisation's products, prices, distribution system, and so on.

c) *Sales Talk*: In traditional marketing jargon, the term "personal selling" is usually cited as an element of the promotional mix. But in the literal sense, the term is only a convenient misnomer because it implies "selling a product in person" rather than through marketing intermediaries like wholesalers and retailers; in other words, it literally refers to the activity of taking a product to a prospective buyer rather than the promotional effort (which is the pertinent element here) that may accompany the activity. For this reason, the term "sales talk" is used in this book and is defined as a promotional tool employed by sales persons to arouse buyers' interest in a product at retail outlets or during telemarketing or personal (that is, customer-to-customer) selling efforts.

Ordinarily, the "sales talk" should particularly involve the provision of information about a given product's advantages over other similar products and its unique attributes, if any. Also, a product's price compared to other products' prices should be highlighted, especially if it is relatively lower. Other aspects that may be brought out in the sales talk may include the buyer's freedom to exchange a product bought for another, or seek reimbursement, if the product does not measure up to the claimed or expected quality or standard. This can promote sales especially if competitors do not give such freedom to customers.

d) *Impulsive Mail*: In a highly competitive socio-economic setting, such as that obtaining in such free market societies as the United States of America, some organisations engage in a form of promotional campaign which involves "scatter-mailing" a mass of standardised mail containing information on, say, new product offerings, quantity discounts, price and/or cash discounts, and/or professional services to potential customers. Addresses for the potential customers are obtainable from various sources, such as the following: post office listings of renters of mail boxes, and lists of subscribers to journals, magazines, newspapers, and the like. Sometimes the standardised mail is addressed to target customer groups using such epithetical terms as "The Resident," "The Occupant," "The Tenant," "The Proprietor," and the like.

This mode of promoting an organisation's sales (which, in treatises and at colloquia on marketing, is commonly distinguished from other promotional efforts by the somewhat mute term "direct mail") is referred to as "impulsive mail" in this book. The mail is designated as being "impulsive" because targeted potential customers often find it difficult to resist, since it generally carries very attractive (although deceptive at times) price discounts, "money-back" guarantees, "no-obligation" pledges, free samples, gifts accompanying each purchase made, and so on.

It should perhaps be noted in passing that this form of marketing communication has, by and large, been cited and blamed by some environmentalists as being responsible for much of the "junk mail" littering many of the world's big cities today. Some recipients of "random" mail have misgivings about such mail and, as such, discard it upon receipt. This is particularly true for misdirected impulsive mail.

e) *Emissary-Style Promotion*:  Some organisations employ a sales-promoting strategy that cannot be easily classified under any of the promotional tools discussed above. This strategy involves such corporate efforts as the following: (i) encouraging managers and the rank and file to use their organisation's products at work and after work by offering them "staff discounts" on purchases of the products, and/or regularly giving them free products; and (ii) instilling in them a sense of pride in the organisation's products, as well as encouraging them to talk positively about the organisation's products. Unlike the other promotional tools which are normally the preserve of marketing departments, this promotional method is basically an organisation-wide effort which requires the involvement of all organisational members. For lack of a better and more precise term, I have referred to this sales-promoting effort as "emissary-style promotion," and have defined it thus:

> A sales-getting tool used by some organisations involving the deliberate use of their managers and workers to promote the organisations' products by using the products, as well as talking positively about them, during work and after-work situations.

Certainly, managers and workers have much to gain by accepting to be used as "ambassadors of goodwill" for their organisation's products. They would, no doubt, value their association with an organisation that has exceptional and reputable profit-earning power. Also, they would definitely share in their organisation's resulting successes through improved conditions of employment and enhanced job security. And, after all, workers and managers should contribute toward their organisation's corporate effort at ensuring protracted, long-term profitability; they should, among other things, be fully involved in such sales-promoting drives as "emissary-style promotion." Would it not, for example, be damaging to an auto-maker whose workers and managers are usually seen driving competitors' automobiles by prospective buyers? What would be more telling about the quality of a company's products than the apparent taste for, or against, them shown by those who are directly involved in making them?

f) *Customer Relations*: The term "customer relations" refers to an organisation's planned effort aimed at creating and maintaining a positive interaction between the organisation and its customers, who are apparently the most essential publics for any given organisation. Essentially, "customer relations"[33] is a deliberate effort aimed at gathering and analysing information about customers' feelings and complaints regarding an organisation's marketing mix, and then taking the necessary measures to preclude widespread customer discontent that can evoke high-spirited consumerism.

Unlike the other sales-getting efforts discussed briefly in the foregoing paragraphs, customer relations clearly requires the *active* involvement of the external parties who constitute an organisation's clientele. For this reason, the customer relations effort is discussed in greater detail in Chapter 4 as one of the essential elements of an organisation's dealings with external parties.

2) THE MARKETING COMMUNICATION PROCESS. The major elements of the marketing communication process, which are diagrammatically portrayed in Figure 2.3, are as follows: the marketer, the communication media, the target market, and the communication results. These elements are briefly described in the ensuing sections.

a) THE MARKETER. The "marketer" represents the source or origin of any given organisation's marketing communication attempt. An organisation's marketing manager, product promotion manager, or any other qualified executive with a different designation may assume the responsibility of initiating a marketing communication attempt. The following are the marketer's major tasks or responsibilities in the marketing communication process: identification of product attributes to be communicated to a designated target market, formulation of an appropriate promotional strategy, and preparation of appropriate promotional messages. A brief discussion of each of these responsibilities follows.

Figure 2.3: The Marketing Communication Process

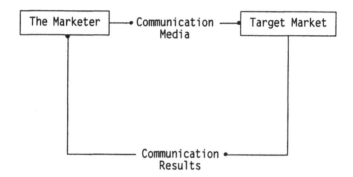

i) *Product Attributes*: The initial step in the marketing communication process is the identification of product attributes that a marketing executive or product promotion manager needs to communicate to a particular customer group. These may include the functional, safety, durability, aesthetic, and other tangible and intangible attributes that make the product concerned distinctively different from products supplied by other organisations. A product's price relative to the prices of other similar products is also an important attribute if it is attractively lower.

ii) *Promotional Strategy*: This step involves the formulation of a promotional plan comprising a set of elements of the promotional mix that are appropriate for communicating the tangible and/or intangible product attributes identified in the foregoing step. The promotional mix elements or variables that marketers may consider here are the following: advertising, publicity, sales talk, emissary-style promotion, impulsive mail, and customer relations.

iii) *Promotional Message*: At this stage, the marketer should prepare the appropriate promotional messages for each sales-getting tool in the promotional plan designed in the foregoing step of the marketing communication process. As much as possible, the messages should carry the distinctive attributes of an organisation's products rather than exaggerated, misleading, or false statements. In other words, marketers should avoid using such crude messages as "best selling car," "number 1 selling detergent," and the like, if such claims cannot be proved easily; buyers are more generally interested in specific benefits they should expect to derive from the purchase of a product than the fact that a particular product is the "best" or "number 1" selling product *per se*.

It is important to prepare several designs or formats for presenting any given promotional message so that each format can be presented every other time the promotional message is featured to guard against monotony. Protracted presentation of a promotional message in the same format to any given audience or target market can very easily cause a feeling of displeasure and aversion, which may eventually culminate in negative feelings and attitudes toward both the promotional message and the product involved.

b) COMMUNICATION MEDIA. Once the appropriate promotional messages are prepared for each sales-getting element in the promotional strategy, the next step should be the selection of appropriate communication media. The following are among the commonly used promotional communication media, albeit the use of any of them will, by and large, be dictated by the nature of the promotional element involved: directories, newspapers, magazines, catalogues, journals, word-of-mouth, television, radio, caps and T-shirts, billboards, point-of-sale posters, and so forth.

c) THE TARGET MARKET. The "target market" is the intended audience for any given organisation's marketing communication attempt. For this reason, marketers need to consider the following to be able to determine the appropriate product attributes, promotional strategy, and promotional messages: the general socio-cultural values, population sizes, and levels of income of their target markets, as well as the intensity of existing and potential competition in the target markets.

d)  MARKETING COMMUNICATION RESULTS.  The last component of the marketing communication process is the feedback to the origin of the marketing communication attempt, which may take the form of increases in sales volume, positive or negative reactions to the promotional campaign by customers or religious and other groups, and so forth. Marketers should respond promptly to any undesirable consequences of their marketing communication efforts in order to guard against losing customers to competitors.

<><>

# 3/ ORGANISATIONAL COMPETITIVENESS

Thus far, we have explored the basic elements of *the management process* and *business communication* in Chapters 1 and 2, respectively. In this chapter, let us consider managerial imperatives which are fundamental to the creation of competitive organisational entities; these are: motivation of employees, the nurturing of innovation, effective management of change, and cost minimisation. A discussion of each of these imperatives follows.

## 3.1 MOTIVATION OF EMPLOYEES

Managers cannot attain meaningful results through the efforts of others unless they have the ability to induce subordinates to invest their full energies, time, and commitment in work to attain higher levels of performance. As such, managers need to create a work environment that is both interesting and stimulating, that is, an environment that has the potential to elicit employees' desire to contribute fully to organisational success and survival. This can be done in many ways, such as by introducing an incentive scheme that rewards exceptional behaviour and/or performance.

Another practical way of eliciting employees' enthusiasm to work is for supervisory and managerial personnel to gauge the long-term personal goals and aspirations of subordinates earmarked for retention so that management can design a package of fringe benefits that includes special incentives intended to enhance the attainment of their goals and aspirations and optimistically motivate them to contribute meaningfully to the well-being of the organisation. The question to ask such subordinates should be akin to the following: "What can we do for you that will make you consider having a long-term association with our organisation?"

Since no organisation can possibly have unlimited, or an over-abundance of, financial resources to meet employees' demands, it is essential that subordinates are initially apprised of the maximum financial commitment an organisation's top management is willing to make in this endeavour, and the organisation's expectations of subordinates who may avail themselves of its "golden handcuffs."

But regardless of the mode used in inspiring employees to readily whir into action in pursuit of organisational goals, it is essential for an organisation's executives to practise the following if they are to evoke a high level of morale and motivation among their subordinates: (a) keep employees informed on a regular basis about organisational issues, plans and problems that concern them; (b) establish an atmosphere of trust; (c) be empathetic, that is, walk in their shoes, so to speak; (d) listen genuinely to, and act promptly on, their problems and suggestions; and (e) acknowledge and celebrate their individual and/or collective achievements, as well as their overall contribution to organisational well-being.[34] It is also important to note that a superior's enthusiasm to discharge his or her duties can gradually engender a more positive work attitude among subordinates, as well inspire them to contribute more willingly to organisational success and survival.

In the remainder of this section, an attempt is made to provide a concise bird's-eye view of some of the common management theories which executives can consider in their quest to elicit the morale and motivation of organisational members; these are: Maslow's hierarchy of needs, McGregor's Theory X and Theory Y, Herzberg's two-factor theory, Vroom's expectancy model, and Adams' equity theory.

THE HIERARCHY OF NEEDS

This refers to the theory introduced by Abraham Maslow, which classifies human needs in ascending order as follows: (a) *physiological needs*, including the needs for food, water and shelter; (b) *security needs*, that is, the need for both physical and psychological safety and security; (c) *social needs*, including the needs for belonging, affection and affiliation; (d) *esteem needs*, such as the needs for respect, recognition and self-esteem; and (e) *self-actualisation needs*, including the needs for personal accomplishment and self-fulfillment.[35]

According to Maslow, a person is motivated by unsatisfied needs; once such needs are satiated, they cease to function as motivators and the next level of needs subsequently become the determinant of an individual's attitudes and behaviour. The implication of this theory for managers is that they need to provide rewards, as well as create opportunities, that can enable organisational members to progressively satisfy the five categories of needs.

There are a number of practical ways in which managers can do this; for example, physiological needs can very easily be satisfied through the provision of adequate remuneration, since this can enable employees to afford food, shelter, and other basic necessities of life. Provision of greater job security and a safe work environment, on the other hand, can enable organisational members to satisfy their security needs, while compatible peers, a compassionate supervisor and greater opportunities for interaction in the work place can partly facilitate the satisfaction of their social needs.

Esteem needs can be met through promotions, achievement-based pay rises, and praise from superiors in recognition of satisfactory or exceptional performance. The satisfaction of self-actualisation needs can be facilitated by interesting and challenging work, as well as a greater degree of autonomy in discharging one's formal duties.

THEORY X AND THEORY Y

The term "Theory X" represents a set of views or assumptions that portray human beings as being naturally lazy, disinterested in achievement, resentful of responsibility, and, among other things, as lacking integrity. "Theory Y," on the other hand, is a set of contrary views or assumptions about the nature of human beings. Both Theory X and Theory Y were postulated by Douglas McGregor,[36] who maintained that the manner in which superiors treat their subordinates in organisational settings is largely a function of the views or assumptions they hold about the nature of human beings.

There is no doubt that the manner in which subordinates are treated by their superiors can affect the degree of their willingness and enthusiasm to work. It should be common knowledge, for example, that a manager who is Theory X oriented and conceives of people as being naturally lazy, disinterested in achievement, resentful of responsibility, and lacking integrity will turn his or her underlings into lethargic, less-creative, and rebellious individuals through strict supervision and rigid work rules and regulations.

A Theory Y manager, on the other hand, will generally turn his or her subordinates into enthusiastic and committed performers through participative decision making and relaxed supervision and work rules. This should be expected considering the fact that employees who are treated as mature, responsible, and dutiful people will generally tend to conduct themselves as such.

### THE TWO-FACTOR THEORY

This theory, which is also sometimes referred to as the "motivation-hygiene theory," was introduced by Frederick Herzberg. Essentially, the theory is explained in terms of two sets of factors. These are: "job content" factors, which are directly related to the job itself and are also sometimes referred to as *motivators* or *satisfiers*; and "job context" factors, which are basically aspects that are peripheral to the job itself and are sometimes alternatively referred to as dissatisfiers, hygiene factors, or maintenance factors. The *content* factors are as follows: the work itself, achievement, recognition, responsibility, advancement, and personal growth. *Context* factors, on the other hand, are: company policy and administration, supervision, working conditions, interpersonal relations, salary or wages, status, job security, and personal life.[37]

According to Herzberg, the presence of *content* factors leads to job satisfaction among employees, while the absence of such factors results in *no* job satisfaction rather than in dissatisfaction. And the presence of *context* factors results in *no* job dissatisfaction rather than in job satisfaction, while the absence of these maintenance factors culminates in job dissatisfaction among employees. What this implies is that both *content* and *context* factors need to be fully addressed by management, but only the former should be expected to motivate employees to contribute meaningfully to organisational success; the latter, that is, "context" factors, need to be addressed mainly for the purpose of forestalling job dissatisfaction among organisational members.

## THE EXPECTANCY MODEL

Vroom has theorised that an employee's motivation to work is a function of three factors; these are: (a) the probability that one's effort can actually lead to the attainment of a stipulated performance target (expectancy); (b) the probability that attainment of the stipulated performance target can lead to a particular reward, such as a promotion or a pay raise (instrumentality); and (c) the value or importance a person attaches to the reward (valence).[38] Without having to delve into the rigour of the model, let us consider how a manager can use it to elicit employees' motivation to work.

Each of the three factors cited in the foregoing paragraph can be influenced by an organisation's management in a number of ways. Employees' *expectancies*, for instance, can be improved greatly by introducing a formal training and development programme, generation of realistic and achievable performance targets, furnishing employees with clear job descriptions, and making adequate resources and support services available to employees. To influence *instrumentality*, managers need to ensure that performance targets and the specific rewards or incentives associated with satisfactory attainment of the targets are clearly and fully communicated to each and every organisational member, particularly and preferably during the employee orientation process.

And, with respect to *valence*, managers in various units of an organisation can annually request their subordinates to suggest and rank the kinds of incentives they would prefer if they achieved stipulated performance targets, so that top management can use the suggestions to design an incentive scheme that is consistent with the general expectations of organisational members.

## EQUITY THEORY

Essentially, this theory assumes that people's tendency to compare themselves with others leads to perceptions of *equity* and *inequity* in organisational settings. According to Stacy Adams, the pundit who developed the theory,[39] a perception of equity occurs when the rewards an employee receives for his or her work inputs compare favourably with the rewards and work inputs of other employees within or outside his or her employer-organisation who hold a similar job. Inequity, on the other hand, is perceived when one feels that the rewards one gets for one's work inputs are either greater or less than the rewards others get for their work inputs.

The "rewards" alluded to here may include basic pay, fringe benefits and praise or recognition from management, while the "work inputs" which an employee may regard as being important may include work experience, educational attainments, training, skills, seniority, the amount of risk involved in one's work, the amount of mental and/or physical effort needed in performing work, the quantity and/or quality of output produced, *et cetera*.

Algebraically, perceptions of equity and inequity may be portrayed as follows:

$$\text{Equity:} \qquad \frac{R_1}{I_1} = \frac{R_2}{I_2}$$

$$\text{Inequity:} \qquad \frac{R_1}{I_1} < \frac{R_2}{I_2}$$

or

$$\frac{R_1}{I_1} > \frac{R_2}{I_2}$$

where

$R_1/I_1$ is the ratio of rewards to work inputs for a

particular employee; and

$R_2/I_2$ is the ratio of rewards to work inputs for another employee or a group of employees that is the object of comparison.

Equity theory predicts that employees who may perceive an imbalance between their work effort and emoluments and the work effort and emoluments of other employees of similar standing within or outside their organisations that is in their favour (that is, $R_1/I_1 > R_2/I_2$) are likely to have greater job satisfaction and an enhanced desire to increase their levels of performance. Perceived equity (that is, $R_1/I_1 = R_2/I_2$) is also likely to improve both job satisfaction and performance.

On the other hand, employees who may perceive an imbalance that is not in their favour (that is, $R_1/I_1 < R_2/I_2$) are likely to engage in the following kinds of behaviour: (a) strive to get the imbalance removed by openly confronting their superiors to redress the situation; (b) deliberately reducing their level of performance; (c) engage in self-remuneration activities, such as pilfering; (d) decide to tolerate the imbalance; or (e) quit working for the organisation.

It should be emphasised here that the imbalance which may evoke the foregoing kinds of behaviour will generally be "perceived" rather than real, and will often be a result of lack of information about an organisation's reward system, particularly with respect to pay scales and incentive schemes for various categories of jobs and work units. It is, therefore, important for managers to ensure that organisational members are adequately informed about wages, salaries, and fringe benefits, and how these may apply to, or differ among, various work units and job categories. The purpose for doing all this is to ensure that organisational members' morale and motivation are not dampened by perceived or imagined inequity in conditions of employment.

*Other Factors.* Besides an individual's willingness and enthusiasm to work (that is, *motivation*), there are obviously other factors which have an important bearing on the level of each individual employee's performance. Ivancevich and Matteson have identified such other factors as the *capacity* to perform (which is a function of the level of an individual's job-related knowledge, skills and experience), and the *opportunity* to perform (which relates to the availability of support and resources needed in performing work).[40] (Note: What Ivancevich and Matteson have referred to as "the opportunity to work" may perhaps have been intended to imply "a supportive work environment.")

### 3.2 QUEST FOR INNOVATION

Today's businesses are operated in very volatile market, social, economic, and other environments. This aspect has created a need for business executives to possess an aptitude in innovation in order for them to be able to adapt their organisations' strategies and operations to the demands of rapidly changing conditions. After all, business managers are supposed to be change agents; and because change is generally inevitable, managers are not likely to succeed in their pursuits and endeavours if they cannot change their business philosophies, strategies and outlooks to be able to cope with business downturns, as well as to benefit from business upswings.

In addition to possessing a spirit for innovation, managers need to encourage each and every organisational member to suggest new ideas which can benefit their organisations through reduced operational and maintenance costs, improved quality and quantity of product offerings, improved administrative efficiency, and increased organisation-wide commitment to attain greater levels of performance. Some of the viable initiatives which managers may need to introduce in their organisations include the following: a gripe system, a "ringi" decision-making system, an open-door policy, and quality circles. A brief description of each of these initiatives follows.

1) GRIPE SYSTEM. This initiative requires a business organisation to introduce a system for gauging employees' innovative ideas and suggestions. Such a system should be operated by means of suggestion boxes and an employee "hot line" through which organisational members can anonymously or otherwise suggest changes that can benefit the organisation. An important requirement here is for management to promptly analyse and, if feasible, implement suggested changes in order to build employees' trust in the organisation's inten-

tions for initiating such a system.

2) RINGI SYSTEM. The "ringi" system is a Japanese decision-making system in which an organisation encourages individual middle-level managers to generate or suggest innovative ideas and prepare a plan or proposal (referred to as a *ringisho*) on how the ideas can be implemented to the benefit of the organisation. The system may be described in a nutshell as follows: first, the written proposal, or "ringisho," is initially circulated among the sponsor's peers for examination and comments; and, second, the "ringisho" is sent to the organisation's top management for evaluation and possible approval for implementation either as suggested by the sponsor or with some suggested modifications by the sponsor's peers.

3) OPEN-DOOR POLICY. This strategy requires the top management of an organisation to generate a formal policy that encourages managers, administrators and supervisors to adopt an open-door posture so that the rank and file can freely call upon them any time to suggest or discuss ways in which quality, productivity, work-related stress, employee morale, and so forth, can be improved.

4) QUALITY CIRCLES. This is a Japanese management practice that essentially provides for work groups to meet regularly (say, once every month) on company time to critically discuss production and/or operational problems and how the existing *modus operandi* can be altered to yield improved performance.[41]

*Conclusion.* Obviously, each of the foregoing schemes requires an atmosphere of openness and trust. To create such a work environment, managers need to avoid playing "favourites," among other things, as this can ruin team spirit - or *espri de corps*,[42] to use one of Fayol's fourteen principles of management - in the work place; moreover, they need to advise subordinates to desist from gossiping about other employees' performance and/or private matters as this can eventually result in conflict and bickering in the work place and consequently thwart the potential for innovation among organisational members.

An important tenet to remember here is that innovation, as Rapp and Collins have maintained, is never out of style; there are always better ways of doing things waiting to be discovered by those who dare to reach beyond what is already known and tried.[43] At Chipco in the United States, an anonymous manager has provided a characterisation of his employer-organisation that is befitting of an organisation which has a genuine desire for innovation:

> *We're a proposal-oriented company; even the janitor*
> *can make a proposal and it will be seriously consid-*
> *ered.*[44]

## 3.3 MANAGEMENT OF CHANGE[45]

Among the most important tasks which managers are expected to perform is making decisions concerning various aspects, issues, and problems of their organisations' product offerings. The outcomes of the decision-making process, that is, decisions, are normally about *changes* from an existing, less-desirable situation toward a more desirable state of being. Unfortunately, though, necessary changes in the operations of some organisations are either not initiated (due to what Silver and Mitchell have referred to as "the status quo tendency"[46]) or are poorly implemented. The status quo tendency in decision making, as Silver and Mitchell have theorised, manifests itself in resistance to change among business executives and, thus, makes those who are trapped in it to continue to pursue existing goals and plans even though the turbulent and complex nature of today's business milieu requires them to make regular changes in the operations of their organisations.

However, even a passion for change on the part of an organisation's executives may not be beneficial to the organisation unless the change process is skilfully managed. This means that change initiators have to guard against instituting organisational changes haphazardly. In other words, they should learn to introduce changes systematically. As an initial step, they need to have a clear visualisation of the change process. In this book, the change process is conceived of as comprising the following elements: triggers of change, a programme for change, implementation of proposed change, evaluation of the effects of the change, and, if need arises, a revision of both the programme for change and the implementation process. These elements are depicted in Figure 3.1 and briefly described in the ensuing paragraphs.[47]

Figure 3.1: The Change Process

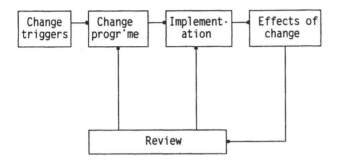

TRIGGERS OF CHANGE. The need for change can be evoked by either internal or external triggers. *Internal triggers* may take the form of such factors as employee demands or complaints, observed administrative or operational problems, or a passion for change on the part of management. *External triggers*, on the other hand, may take the form of factors like customer complaints or protests, competitive pressures, and/or changes in economic conditions, consumer tastes or government legislation.

CHANGE PROGRAMME. The programme for change is basically a plan of action and should essentially provide the following: (a) well-reasoned answers to the five questions raised elsewhere in this section; and (b) specifics pertaining to such aspects as time limits within which the change is to be implemented, personnel responsibilities, sourcing and financing of needed resources, tangible and intangible benefits expected to accrue from the change, and so forth.

CHANGE IMPLEMENTATION. Once a programme for change has been designed, implementation of the envisaged change should promptly follow. This requires managers to perform certain administrative and supervisory chores, such as motivating employees, maintaining discipline among employees, coordinating the activities of employees and work units, and the like.

EVALUATION OF EFFECTS. After the introduction of proposed change, management needs to periodically assess its effects. If there are no serious negative effects each time the assessment is undertaken, the implementation process should go on without any interruption. However, if the assessment reveals any serious unexpected effects, a *review* and refinement of both the change programme and the implementation process should be made promptly.

Besides the need for managers to have a clear visualisation of the change process, change initiators, as Theodore Herbert has advised, need to ask and fully answer the ensuing questions before they decide to introduce any envisaged change:[48]

1) Is the change necessary? In other words, is the change likely to bring about greater returns than the costs of implementing it?

2) Is the change the correct one, or are alternative change programmes likely to yield greater and more desirable end results for the business?

3) What are the likely negative impacts of the change on other spheres and operations of the business? Are these impacts likely to offset the benefits to be gained from the change?

4) How will acceptance of the change by those who are likely to be affected by it either directly or otherwise be secured?

5) After the envisaged change has been implemented, what follow-up will be necessary to ensure that maximum results or benefits accrue from it?

Once the foregoing questions are fully answered and a decision is make in favour of envisaged change, change initiators need to incorporate several touchstones into the change process; these are: genuine participation in the implementation process by employees who are likely to be affected by the change, effective communication by the change initiator, and empathy on the part of the change initiator.[49] A brief discussion of each of these touchstones follows.

PARTICIPATION. Employees who are likely to be affected by change need to be given an opportunity to participate in planning its scope and implementation. This, as Kouzes and Posner have maintained, can enable management to inspire a shared vision among organisational members.[50]

EFFECTIVE COMMUNICATION. Open, two-way communication between the change initiator and employees who are likely to be affected by planned changes is a critical element in the change process. There is no doubt that effective communication about envisaged changes greatly reduces employees' natural resistance to change by clearing any fears, doubts and suspicions about the intentions and likely effects of planned change programmes. Unless an organisation's internal setting provides for open, two-way communication among employees and work units, therefore, change programmes which may be introduced in such an organisation are likely to nurture conflict, resentment and sabotage.

EMPATHY. There is also a need for management folk to put themselves in their subordinates' shoes, so to speak. Unless they are empathetic, they cannot possibly understand and work to reduce the anxieties and sentiments of those who are likely to be affected by the changes they may seek to introduce.

## 3.4 COST MINIMISATION

Most managers, as Alvin Toffler has observed, are inclined to pursue business as usual even when they are warned of impending upheaval, and despite the fact that "business as usual is dangerous in an environment that has become, for all practical purposes, permanently convulsive."[51] In the 21st century and beyond, these complacent and conservative kinds of managers Toffler has alluded to should not wonder when what have so far proved to be viable strategies for their organisations turn out to be tragedies at best.

Nevertheless, what should be the strategies and imperatives for managers in the kind of socio-economic setting described in the foregoing section? The following are among the obvious of the many viable strategies which executives need to address themselves to: streamlining their operations, being innovative (this is the subject of discussion of Section 3.2), simplifying product designs, sourcing cheaper inputs, and engaging in collaborative product promotions.[52] Each of these strategies and imperatives is discussed in a nutshell below.

### STREAMLINING OPERATIONS

Inflationary trends in much of the world today have led to an erosion of buyers' purchasing power, a situation which has posed significant problems for business undertakings in their marketing efforts. To be able to sell their goods and/or services to attain profitable sales levels for their organisations, therefore, managers need to streamline their operations to minimise operational costs. This should enable them to charge lower prices that are within the reach of consumers, whose purchasing power has been declining rapidly over the last several years. Managers should sell the streamlining idea to other units in their organisations to achieve even greater cost minimisation.

### SIMPLIFIED PRODUCT DESIGNS

To provide maximum value to customers at minimum cost, managers need to identify superfluous features of products and recommend to design engineers to exclude such features. The simplification of product designs can, in turn, result in simplified production processes. In all likelihood, this can eventually result in reduced costs of production and improve executives' ability to charge lower prices. Managers should, however, ensure that the simplification of product designs does not reduce the functionality and quality of products concerned. As much as possible, the functional, quality, and aesthetic attributes of product offerings should be maintained to ensure that customer satisfaction is not sacrificed.

Simply stated, simplifying product designs (or, more precisely, design simplification) essentially involves eliminating unnecessary features of products in order to minimise costs of production while maintaining, or even increasing, customer satisfaction.[53]

### SOURCING CHEAPER INPUTS

Managers should also strive to reduce unnecessary expenditures associated with purchased production materials and machinery and equipment. This can be accomplished in many ways. One way is to carefully study the purpose served by each production input and find substitute and less costly inputs that would adequately serve the same purpose. Another way is to source less costly materials, machinery and equipment that are available locally or in neighbouring countries. All these efforts require a great deal of innovation and flexibility among executives and their organisations.

The foregoing may be stated a bit differently in terms of *value engineering* for the benefit of students of operations and production management as follows: there is a need to analyse the specifications of purchased materials, parts, machinery, and products to determine whether or not less costly alternatives can be found and used in their place without reducing the quality of a company's work and/or outputs.

### COLLABORATIVE PRODUCT PROMOTIONS

The term "collaborative product promotion" may be defined to refer to a promotional strategy whereby two or more suppliers of, say, complementary goods or any other kinds of non-substitute goods jointly design and launch a single promotional campaign for a selected number of their product offerings. For example, a bread supplier and a supplier of butter may jointly design and launch a single promotional campaign for the two classes of products. This is advantageous in that collaborating companies can share the cost of promotional campaigns. Moreover, there is an additional benefit that may accrue to an organisation seeking to engage in collaborative or joint promotional efforts: if collaborating companies have developed sound public and customer relations, there is no doubt that the organisation can greatly benefit from the reputation and goodwill of such companies.

# 4/ DEALINGS WITH EXTERNAL PARTIES

Two elements constitute every organisation's dealings with external parties; these are: *customer* relations and *public* relations. The first element, that is, "customer relations," concerns an organisation's dealings with those external parties who make up its clientele and typically falls under the auspices of marketing departments. "Public relations," on the other hand, pertains to an organisation's dealings with external stakeholders other than its customers and is normally a corporate-level function. These two important elements of an organisation's dealings with external parties are the focus of this chapter.

## 4.1 CUSTOMER RELATIONS

To reiterate, the term "customer relations" may be defined to refer to an organisation's planned effort aimed at creating and maintaining a positive interaction between the organisation and its *customers,* who are apparently among the most essential publics for any given business organisation. Essentially, customer relations[54] is a deliberate effort at gathering and analysing information about customers' feelings and complaints regarding an organisation's marketing mix, that is, its products, costing or pricing structure, promotional activities, and/or distribution system - and taking the necessary measures that will minimise any possible dissatisfaction among customers.

Business organisations should engage in customer relations for the following reasons: (a) it is morally the right thing to do; (b) to gain

75

reputation and protracted goodwill; (c) to prevent the possible loss of customers to existing and/or potential competitors; (d) to encourage the flow of information from customers, which can be useful in improving the organisation's marketing mix; and (e) to prevent any possibility of dissatisfied customers seeking legal action.

In the majority of business organisations in developing economies, the customer relations effort receives very little attention, if any at all. This is especially true among monopolistic state companies, whose customers have very limited choice with respect to variety, quality, and prices of products. Such companies are not generally responsive to customers' desires or reactions mainly because they are assured of a market even in the face of excessive customer dissatisfaction.

Customers' complaints come in different forms and with varying degrees of importance. Common complaints may include customers' expressed dissatisfaction regarding any aspect of a given organisation's marketing mix. There is, of course, no single organisation in the world today that does not evoke customer complaints about any of its marketing mix elements. This is to be expected as it is not possible for any organisation to produce a product that can adequately satisfy the divergent expectations, desires, interests, and perceptions of customers.

The customer relations task should be performed systematically; first, an organisation's customer relations manager needs to gauge customers' attitudes and complaints. Second, customers' attitudes and complaints should be analysed to determine their probable impacts on the organisation's marketing programme. Finally, corrective measures should be taken in order to contain customer discontent. These three steps, which are portrayed in the model in Figure 4.1, are discussed in the remainder of this section. The model depicts the customer relations effort as a continuous process. The customer relations manager should continuously gauge customers' attitudes and complaints, analyse their significance, and take appropriate measures that will forestall or resolve customers' dissatisfaction with any given aspect of an organisation's marketing programme.

1) GAUGING ATTITUDES AND COMPLAINTS.  There are several methods in which customers' complaints or attitudes about an organisation's marketing mix can be gauged; they include field research, suggestion boxes, and customer hot lines. A brief description of each of these

three methods follows.

a) *Field Research:*[55] This can be accomplished in a number of ways. One of the simplest ways is to question customers directly about their feelings or complaints regarding the organisation's marketing mix. This may be done at the point of sale or at other convenient places.

Figure 4.1: A Customer Relations Model

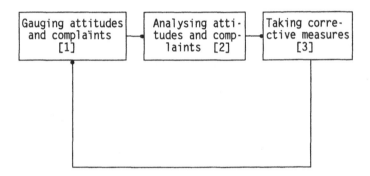

b) *Suggestion Boxes:* Customers' attitudes and complaints can also be known through the use of suggestion boxes, which may be placed at points of sale. Also, special post office boxes may be rented for this purpose; information about the boxes should be disseminated through the press to ensure maximum utilisation of the boxes by customers. The special mail boxes should be checked regularly if the organisation is to respond promptly to the serious complaints or feelings of customers.

c) *Customer Hot Line:* Further, customers' feelings and complaints can be received through a customer hot line, which may be installed for customers to make telephone calls directly to the supplier.[56] Like suggestion boxes, the customer hot line should also be publicised through the mass media if it is to be used to the maximum. Complaints or feelings expressed through the hot line should be promptly analysed and attended to in order to build customers' trust in the organisation's intentions for providing such a facility.

2) EVALUATING ATTITUDES AND COMPLAINTS. Once customers' complaints and/or attitudes are known, the next step should be to evaluate them in terms of their probable impact on the success of the organisation's marketing programmes. This should guide the customer relations manager in ranking the complaints or attitudes according to their significance on the success of the organisation's marketing activities.

3) TAKING CORRECTIVE MEASURES. The evaluation of customers' attitudes and complaints should lead to the taking of remedial measures to mitigate dissatisfaction caused by any given aspects of an organisation's marketing mix. Priority in doing this should be given to the most serious attitudes and complaints to prevent widespread negative publicity. If this is not timely done, the organisation's image is likely to be tarnished by dissatisfied customers, placing its survival and success at stake.

The kinds of corrective measures an organisation can take depends on the nature of the problems causing discontent. For example, if a religious grouping complains about some apparent immorality depicted in an advertisement, the appropriate business action should be to withdraw the advertisement. If the complaint is about a product's poor quality, the producer should strive to improve the quality of the product, or charge a lower price that matches the relative quality of the product.

*Proactive Strategy.* In addition to the reactive approach of taking corrective measures to quench customers' expressed complaints or feelings, an organisation can design a programme that can reduce the incidence of such complaints and feelings. Such a programme may consist of the following, among other things: product warranties, product recalls, and honest promotional activities.

a) *Warranties*: Business organisations whose products are technically complex need to provide express warranties to buyers of such products. In other words, suppliers should give written or verbal statements indicating that they would repair or replace items (at no extra cost or at a nominal charge) that might malfunction without the buyers' fault within a stipulated period of time.

b) *Product Recalls*: Organisations whose products may be found to be hazardous or unworthy should voluntarily recall all such products and repair, replace, or destroy them, depending upon the nature of the problem. Products recalled could be with consumers or middlemen (that is, wholesalers, retailers, and so on). Whoever is in possession of such products should be notified promptly through the mass media about the nature of the problem so that they can return them to designated dealers or depots with minimum delay.

c) *Honest Promotional Activities*: Business organisations need to avoid exaggerated product claims, misleading statements, and half-truths in their promotional messages. Deceptive promotional activities can be a source of legal implications or widespread dissatisfaction among customers when products fail to meet expectations evoked by sellers' false or exaggerated claims regarding the products' attributes.

*Benefits.* In all probability, a programme consisting of the foregoing three business initiatives can greatly mitigate the number of complaints and the depth of negative feelings and attitudes regarding an organisation and its marketing mix. In fact, these initiatives can also greatly contribute to the enhancement of an organisation's public image and competitive posture. Even product recalls which may often result in heavy financial losses can be justified by the enhanced public image and business goodwill that usually accrue from such action, and which can generally offset any possible losses in the short term.

In the next section, we are going to survey the second element of an organisation's dealings with external parties, that is *public relations*. In the meantime, let us digress somewhat and briefly discuss an equally important subject for modern managers, that is, *customer satisfaction*.

CUSTOMER SATISFACTION. Can anyone think of a business statement, premise, concept, or philosophy which can be widely accepted as a manager's creed? What has been discussed thus far about customer relations seems to suggest that, if anything has a chance of being generally embraced as a business manager's creed, it can only be the following statement:

I BELIEVE THE CUSTOMER IS KING OR QUEEN

But whether or not this postulate can be accepted without having to engage in polemics, one cannot perhaps dismiss the fact that customers' satisfaction with an organisation's product offerings is the basis of sustained repeat sales, as well as enhanced customer referrals. There is no doubt that the long-term viability of a business, any business, is contingent upon its ability to satisfactorily meet the divergent needs and expectations of its customers. For those who like arithmetic without the use of numbers, this axiom may be expressed simply as follows:

CUSTOMER SATISFACTION = BUSINESS SUCCESS + SURVIVAL

In short, business success in the 21st century, as Bagley and Reese have asserted, is going to be increasingly based on long-term customer satisfaction, which, as maintained earlier, leads to an increase in both referrals and repeat sales.[57] This should provide a compelling reason for managers and their organisations to constantly remind their employees in information flyers (which may be regularly appended to, say, pay slips or stubs) to embrace and act on the "Thou shall not disappoint a customer" commandment. At Sears, Roebuck and Company in the United States, where top management requires each and every employee to provide, and/or to support the provision of, what the retail company has referred to as "outrageous customer service" anchored by a "passion for the customer"), the quest for enhanced, long-term customer satisfaction is facilitated by the use of Town Hall Meetings:[58]

> *In an effort to improve customer service, Sears [Roebuck and Company] holds regular Town Hall Meetings to get ... employees' insights and suggestions. Employees are encouraged to point out barriers they encounter when trying to serve shoppers, and [to suggest] potential solutions.*[59]

A major requirement in the customer satisfaction drive is for management to empower employees to autonomously make certain decisions intended to forestall any potential customer discontent. Moreover, it is important to institute a system for evaluating how well employees - particularly sales personnel - are contributing to the customer satisfaction drive, as well provide the necessary incentives for exceptional performance in this regard.

The *employee assessment* exercise may be accomplished through a combination of evaluations made by company-sponsored mystery shoppers and supervisors' appraisals. The following questions, among others, should aid managers in the determination of useful criteria to be employed in the evaluation exercise: Does he or she dress in an appropriate manner? Does he or she serve customers promptly? Does he or she provide service with courtesy? And does he or she seem to have adequate knowledge of product features and the benefits of such features to customers?

A package of *incentives* for exceptional performance may include the following: certificates of recognition, money, special name tags, commendation letters from top management, inclusion of superior performers in a company's television and newspaper commercials, and/or inscription of employees' names on plaques to be displayed on walls of lobbies or hallways. These incentives can be disbursed annually or on a more regular basis.

An additional element to remember here is that customer satisfaction cannot easily be achieved unless the activities of customer relations and/or sales personnel are periodically monitored, appraised and controlled by top management. The following remarks made by an IBM chief executive officer about customer complaints should underscore the need for top management to actively monitor, appraise and control the customer relations effort or any semblance thereof: "I am sick and tired of ... hear[ing] nothing but great things about quality and cycle times, and then to visit customers who tell me of problems."[60]

It is also important for managers to realise that the growing emphasis on  pronounced customer service as a critical factor in the long-term success and survival of a business is rapidly conditioning customers to expect much, much more than just the goods and/or services that may be on offer. Those who pay only lip-service to customer service, as well as those who consciously or otherwise avoid it altogether, should, therefore, not be surprised if and when they fall by the wayside.

Finally, managers who wish to attain better than marginal results in the years ahead would do well to ask themselves and answer the

following questions suggested by Rapp and Collins:[61] Are we identifying and contacting our best prospects and customers? Are we ready
to invest in exceeding customer expectations without a guarantee of
an immediate payback? Are we courting each individual prospect and
customer as if our company's future depends on it? And are we
identifying the segments and niches within our database that are ideal
for targeted promotional campaigns and/or new product offerings?

## 4.2 PUBLIC RELATIONS

The term "public relations" is used in this book to refer to those
communications and other organisational efforts and activities which
are intended to promote and maintain harmonious relations between
an organisation and the external groups that have a stake in the
organisation's corporate policies, programmes, and overall existence.[62] The ultimate responsibility for good public relations with all
major segments of an organisation's public rests directly and entirely
with the officer appointed to function as the organisation's link with
external parties. Essentially, this means that the public relations officer
needs to devote his or her time to developing and maintaining his or
her organisation's reputation, goodwill, and public image. Figure 4.2
portrays the position on a simplified organisation chart that would be
befitting for the public relations (PR) officer or manager.

### THE MAJOR PUBLICS

The major segments of any given organisation's public are usually
the following: (a) the government; (b) shareholders; (c) host communities; and (d) suppliers. A brief discourse on the need for an organisation to interact positively with each of these various publics follows.
(Note: *employees* are usually treated as a segment of every organisation's public; in this book, however, they are conceived of as a constituent part of an organisation rather than a public).

1) THE GOVERNMENT. Organisations should develop and maintain
satisfactory relations with such governmental units as tax, public
health, and regulatory agencies. Good and amicable relations with

these agencies are likely to lead to the scaling down of governmental surveillance of their activities. Sound relations with local authorities is of equal importance. Such issues as those pertaining to personal levy, trading licences and public health, among a host of other things, should be attended to if a business ever wishes to win the confidence and trust of local authorities.

Figure 4.2:   The Public Relations Position

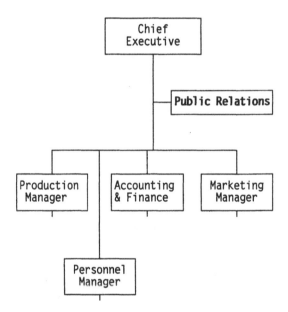

Any organisation whose activities deviate from the expectations and stipulations of the government and local authorities cannot expect to be successful in the long run. The case study on "Mr. Mitchell's Ordeal" at the end of this chapter portrays the critical nature of sound and amicable relations between an organisation and its host government; it features a general manager of a Zambian-based subsidiary of a multinational company, who was reprimanded (by his superiors and government officials) for sending a junior officer to represent the company at a sitting of a commission of inquiry appointed by the government - an action which was interpreted as an overt revelation of his contempt for the Zambian government.

2) SHAREHOLDERS. "Shareholders," also commonly referred to as stockholders, are individuals and/or institutions that own shares of stock in one or more corporations. Ownership of shares of stock in a corporation entitles a shareholder to receive dividends whenever they are declared by the corporation's board of directors. There are generally two classes of stock or shares sold by corporations; these are: common stock, and preferred stock. A brief description of each of these two classes of stock is provided in the ensuing paragraphs.

a) *Common Stock*: This refers to the ordinary shares of a company that carry no special dividend rights or preferential status. There are two forms of common stock, namely, classified common stock and founders' shares. Classified common stock exists in two classes: Class A and Class B. Class A is the common stock normally sold to the public and which typically pays dividends of a consistent amount. Also, it has full voting rights. Class B is normally used by small and new companies seeking to acquire funds from external sources and is usually retained by organisers of a company. Dividends on common stock B are not normally paid until a company has established its earning power.

Founders' shares are like Class B stock in that they do not have the right to dividends for a number of years, but they are unlike class B stock in that they carry sole voting rights.

b) *Preferred Stock*: This is the type of stock whose claims or rights on earnings and/or assets precede those of common stock. What this means is that, when dividends are declared, holders of preferred stock will receive theirs before common stockholders. In the case of assets, it means that preferred stockholders will have preferential claims on the company's assets (while common stock holders will take the residue, if any) in the event of a dissolution of a given corporation. In both cases, however, creditors' claims are ahead of those of both preferred and common stockholders.

*Legal Rights*. Stockholders have several legal rights; they include the following: (a) the right to receive annual reports pertaining to the earnings and operations of the corporation in which they hold shares of stock; (b) the right to inspect the corporation's financial books if they have a legitimate reason for doing so, and if they do not disrupt business operations by so doing; (c) the right to share in the profits of the corporation if dividends are declared; and (d) the right to vote on their organisation's directors and major acquisitions and mergers.[63]

The first shareholders' right cited above, that is, the right to receive *annual reports* about the corporation, is the relevant one for the purposes of this chapter. Annual reports, which are primarily prepared for shareholders, provide information pertaining to the goals, operations, and, among other things, the financial status of a given corporation. To meet the needs of shareholders, therefore, annual reports should include the following: (a) a letter from the chairperson of the corporation's board of directors to shareholders; (b) a list of lawyers, auditors, and/or other external parties that provide professional services to the corporation; (c) financial statements; (d) details on product offerings and markets involved; (e) a statement of efforts intended to minimise costs and/or maximise profits or return on investment; (f) labour-management relations; (g) an assessment of the outlook for the industry in general, and for the corporation in particular; and (h) the corporation's strategies in dealing with any existing and/or potential problems or threats.[64]

3) HOST COMMUNITIES. Since business organisations are a constituent part of the local communities in which they operate, they should logically participate in the various civic activities of those communities. They should, for example, work hand in glove with other institutions in stamping out crime, ridding communities of illegal traders, making charitable contributions to the needy, making the communities habitable, and playing an active role in devising and executing various other social programmes.

All these activities will tend to improve the welfare of the communities in which an organisation's business operations are undertaken. Any organisation that contributes to the improvement of its host community's quality of life will, as a result, have a better community in which to conduct its operations. For example, community improvements may lead to a reduction in such crimes as vandalism, thefts, robberies, and burglaries, which can pose a threat to the survival of any organisational entity. Other benefits of conducting business operations in a community with improved social welfare and a high quality of life include the following: increased labour supply, improved quality of labour, reduced employee attrition, and less absenteeism.

4) SUPPLIERS. Every organisation needs to develop and maintain harmonious relations with suppliers of equipment, raw materials, services, merchandise, capital, and other resources. Such relations, if developed and maintained, can greatly contribute to organisational success. Good relations with suppliers become even more important, and perhaps indispensable, during periods of shortages of whatever is supplied. This does not, however, imply that organisations should engage in unscrupulous dealings in order to obtain the various resources they need, nor does it suggest that suppliers should hoard supplies for "special" orders. Good and acceptable relations with suppliers should thrive on credibility, honesty and fair-play.

### THE PUBLIC RELATIONS MANAGER

The manager or officer who performs the public relations function has a very important role to play; he or she functions as a link between his or her organisation and each of the various segments that constitute the organisation's public. In performing this role, the public relations manager should function as a keen advocate for both the organisation and its various publics. As an advocate for his or her organisation (a role which some people regard as the most important for public relations managers[65]), the public relations manager should competently keep relevant external parties informed about the organisation's *corporate* policies and programmes that are of interest to them. As an advocate for the public, the public relations officer has the task of earnestly apprising organisational members of any existing and/or imminent public relations problems occasioned by the organisation's corporate policies or programmes; also, he or she has to promptly seek the active involvement of organisational members in restoring relations with parties involved.

Figure 4.3 portrays the linking role of public relations managers just described, where *a's* represent an organisation's policies, programmes, and so on, and *b's* the public demands, concerns, protests, and the like, which the organisation has to contend with. Although public relations managers are essentially a part of their organisations' corporate teams, the nature and scope of their job requires them to conceive of themselves as the *medium* through which their organisations and the public can develop and maintain positive relations. To be able to perform this kind of job satisfactorily, it is critical for the public relations practitioner to be aware of the fact that "Basic to the practice of public relations is *effective communications*,"[66] the attainment of which is the primary focus of Section 2.3 in Chapter 2 of this book.

Figure 4.3: The Public Relations Function

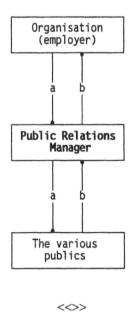

<>

CASE STUDY: MR. MITCHELL'S ORDEAL[67]

Sound relations and interactions between an organisation and the local and/or national governments is essential to enhancing business success, reputation, and goodwill. No organisation is likely to survive in an atmosphere of constant frictions with the government in a country in which it conducts its operations. This fact is clearly implied in the ensuing excerpt from a newspaper article pertaining to the saga of a general manager's "unbecoming" conduct in Zambia:

> *The future of Chloride Zambia general manager, Mr. Jonathan Mitchell, hangs in the balance after his parent company in London disassociated itself from his decision to send a security guard to the tariff commission of inquiry and the commission's chairman rejected his apology to it in Kabwe town. The local board chairman (of his company), Mr. Oliver Irwin, said disciplinary action would have to be taken against Mr. Mitchell as his apology in itself was not sufficient.*
>
> *Both Chloride local board of directors and the London-based group chairman Sir Michael Edwards ... apologised to ... [the Zambian government] for any embarrassment brought about by Mr. Mitchell's conduct. Presenting the two apologies to the tariff commission chairman, Mr. Mark Chona, at the commission's secretariat ... Mr. Irwin said his board wished to sincerely apologise to the ... [government] "for the deplorable manner in which the general manager handled the submission of evidence to your commission."*
>
> *Mr. Chona was ... infuriated by Mr. Mitchell's decision to send a security guard, Mr. Arthur Mweene, to present Chloride Zambia's submission to the commission sitting in Kitwe city. Mr. Chona said Mr. Mitchell's attitude showed the depth of his contempt for the commission appointed by ... [the government].*
>
> *Mr. Mitchell appeared before the commission in Kabwe town several days later to apologise for the incident which he said was an error of judgment on his part and for which he took full personal responsibility. But ... Mr. Chona said the commission had chosen not to ask Mr. Mitchell any questions in Kabwe town because it did not believe his explanation. It was inconceivable that Mr. Mitchell could not find anybody higher than a security guard to represent the company at the commission. The commission did not at any time associate Mr. Mitchell's conduct with either the*

*local or group directorship but understood it to be his own attitude.*

*The apology from the Chloride group chairman was intended to remind ... [the government] of the hitherto good reputation Chloride had enjoyed in Zambia. He felt there had been a misunderstanding in the sense that Mr. Mitchell might have believed a written statement was required when in fact he had to appear in person. In his statement, Mr. Irwin said: "The local board and the international group consider that disciplinary action was essential as an apology itself is inadequate in the circumstances." He said since Mr. Mitchell was a group employee, it would be up to the directors of the group in London to determine the nature of the disciplinary action that would be appropriate.*

**DISCUSSION QUESTIONS**

1) Why do you think Chloride's top management was concerned about Mr. Mitchell's conduct? Discuss.

2) Supposing you were one of the company's influential London-based directors, what disciplinary action against Mr. Mitchell would you have found appropriate for safeguarding the company's good relations with the Zambian government? Explain your answer.

3) In your personal judgment, do you think Mr. Mitchell was treated fairly by the chairman of the tariff commission of inquiry? Discuss.

<>

# 5/ SELF-MANAGEMENT

Let us turn to yet another critical element which managers need to consider if they wish to make success in their managerial pursuits and endeavours nearly as certain as day follows night, so to speak - that is, *self-management*. Essentially, "self-management" involves the following basic activities: managing stress, wise use of one's time, and minding one's health. The remainder of this chapter is devoted to a survey of these three fundamental aspects of self-management.

## 5.1 MANAGING STRESS

The term "stress" refers to the mental, emotional, and/or physical strain or discomfort which an individual may experience due to such factors as the following: (a) unfavourable life experiences like death in one's family or a breakdown in one's valued social or professional relationships, which may affect one's ability to cope with normal work demands; (b) personal incompetence or inability to perform the duties of one's job or position, as postulated by the Peter Principle; and/or (c) organisation-based factors like work overload, interpersonal conflict, poor supervision, and the like.

Stress is generally an inescapable companion in everyone's work life; there is perhaps not a single person who is immune from it. Between hectic work schedules and life's ordinary hassles, no individual, as the Centre for Behavioural Medicine in Denver has observed, can honestly claim not to have ever felt stressed out or anxious at times.[68]

If it reaches excessive levels, stress can be a very unpleasant and debilitating phenomenon; unless individuals learn to effectively cope with it, therefore, it can lead to psychogenic illnesses, poor job performance, and, among other things, chronic employee absenteeism. According to the International Labour Organisation, "stress has become one of the most serious health issues of the 20th century."[69] In the industrialised world particularly, stress-related ailments like ulcers, high blood pressure and heart attacks are so prevalent that they have become a source of great concern. The Japanese have even coined the term "karoshi" to represent stress-related deaths, which have become commonplace in their society in recent years.[70]

Stress-causing factors are not going to be any less impinging on the individual in the 21st century; one's ability to cope with stress is, therefore, going to be one of the benchmarks to an enjoyable and a successful work life in the 21st century.

There is a lot an individual can do in an effort to cope with or reduce stress. One of the initial steps in this endeavour is to identify one's major sources of stress,[71] and then seek to make changes in one's attitudes, behaviour and aspirations that may be contributing to experiences of stress or anxiety. Whatever life-style changes one may make should be complemented by a regimen of personal activities including adequate relaxation, regular exercise, and wise use of one's on-the-job and off-the-job time.

Besides, it is important to set achievable personal and work-related goals for oneself. The basic idea to remember in this regard is the need to avoid biting off more than you can chew, so to speak. If one sets achievable goals and performs tasks without over-stretching one's mental and/or physical capabilities, the risk of experiencing stress can be reduced greatly. Moreover, developing a sense of optimism can partly reduce the effects of stressful life conditions and experiences. As the findings of a recent study conducted in Finland have revealed,[72] optimism can greatly contribute to a reduction in the risk of falling prey to such stress-related ailments as cancer, gastric ulcers, heart attack, high blood pressure, and mental illness.

An individual's superiors can also contribute to the mitigation of stress in a number of ways, such as by designing jobs that provide for greater employee autonomy in planning and executing work, and by involving employees in decision making concerning important departmental and/or organisational matters. And, as *Awake* has advised, managerial and supervisory personnel can greatly contribute to the creation of a less-stressful work environment by being accessible, being good listeners, avoiding the temptation of playing favourites, and by not being sceptical about learning from any of their subordinates who may have constructive ideas which can enhance performance.[73]

## 5.2 WISE USE OF TIME

*Time* is a phenomenon one cannot see, hear, feel, taste, or physically experience, and it is essentially a mysterious and fathomless phenomenon, even to scholars who have pondered and studied it for generations.[74] Perhaps this explains why "time management" pundits avoid delving into defining time in their literary works. In this book, however, an attempt is made to define this historically ineffable phenomenon; it is conceived of as that resource which, unlike other resources, is intangible, cannot be hired, leased, borrowed, lent, or saved, is equally available to everyone, can never be manipulated by anyone, and is an essential ingredient in any given activity.

It is perhaps also important at this juncture to consider why it is important for managers to be conscious of the time element in all their business pursuits and endeavours. Let us turn to James McCay for a quick and apt postulate: "[W]e succeed or fail, not only as business leaders but as human beings, to the extent that we learn how to manage that strangest commodity in the world - time."[75]

Obviously, rational use of time is not an end in itself; as Alec Mackenzie has pointed out, it is a means of enhancing one's overall life in several important ways as follows: (a) it can contribute to the mitigation of *stress*; (b) it can enable a person to achieve a more *balanced life* between work, family and leisure; (c) it can enhance one's *productivity*; and (d) it can enable a person to accomplish both personal and professional *goals*.[76]

### LACK OF TIME CONSCIOUSNESS

Some managers are not time-conscious; while they are excessively conscious of the importance of financial, human, material and other resources in the pursuit of personal and/or organisational goals, they rarely recognise time as a necessary resource which also needs to be taken into account. Obviously, time is a scarce and indispensable element in the attainment of one's stipulated goals. Moreover, time is perhaps the most ungovernable of all resources available to man; it ticks on and on at its own pace regardless of anyone's wishes or abhorrence.

As such, all business pursuits need to be planned and implemented so that they fit into specified time frames if they are to yield any meaningful results. How a business manager uses time at work, therefore, can partly determine his or her level of achievement. Thus, there should be no disputing the fact that unproductive use of time by managers and employees at work can thwart a business's efficiency and effectiveness.

### CAN TIME BE MANAGED?

"Managing Time," "Time Management," the headings tell us. But how accurate are these notions? Can one really manage time? Let us briefly consider the basic functions of *management* as a backdrop in the process of developing a meaningful answer to the question posed here.

The management process, with which the notions "managing time" and "time management" are associated, is accomplished through the performance of the following distinct functions: (a) planning, (b) organising, (c) directing, and (d) controlling.[77] The issue, then, is whether or not managers can really perform the foregoing functions in their dealing with time.

Let us turn to the definition of time tendered earlier for a clue to the right answer: time is that resource which, unlike other resources, is intangible, cannot be hired, leased, borrowed, lent, or saved, is equally available to everyone, can never be manipulated by anyone, and is an essential ingredient in any given activity. The "managing time" and "time management" notions are, therefore, convenient misnomers at best, since no one can actually plan, organise, direct, and/or control time; one can only manage one's affairs "in relation to time."[78] It is for this reason that the heading "Wise Use of Time" is preferred in this book.

In spite of its importance, time does not require one to toil in learning how best to utilise it. All one needs to do are two simple things: first, identify all possible time-wasting activities and, second, avoid these activities as much as possible. Time wasters, as time-conscious executives would probably agree, are numerous. They include the following: lack of priorities, lack of organisation of oneself and/or of one's activities, inability to avoid trivia, unproductive meetings, procrastination, and unclear job descriptions. All these time wasters and tips on how they can be overcome are briefly discussed in the ensuing paragraphs.

1) LACK OF PRIORITIES. Failure to establish priorities can be a serious time waster because it can easily facilitate the spending of valuable time on unnecessary activities. Business people should learn to establish priorities if their time is to be utilised wisely. This may be done simply by classifying work assignments in three categories as follows: (a) *must do* tasks (those that are critical to the operations of the business); (b) *should do* tasks (those which have a lesser priority, but which can become critical if they are not completed); and (c) *nice to do* tasks (those which have no direct bearing on business operations, and which should be attended to only after must do and should do tasks are completed. Obviously, priorities need to be continually reviewed in the light of unexpected circumstances that may require one's prompt attention.

2) LACK OF ORGANISATION. Lack of organisation of oneself and/or of one's work can, in the majority of cases, thwart the attainment of stipulated business goals. Getting organised can be accomplished in many ways, including the following: (a) keeping a list of one's daily tasks; (b) cultivating the necessary commitment and determination to carry out planned work; (c) thinking ahead so as to be able to combine jobs and "kill two or more birds with one stone," so to speak; (d) keeping a neat work place; and (e) guarding against doing too many things at any one particular time.

3) INABILITY TO AVOID TRIVIA. Involving oneself in unimportant matters

at work can lead to necessary tasks not being performed. This must be avoided at all costs. The following are among common trivia that executives and other organisational members should learn to guard against: (a) regular non-business visits at places of work; and (b) unnecessary paperwork, such as that created by communication attempts through letters or memoranda where personal contacts or the telephone could do just as well.

With respect to unsolicited callers, it is prudent to avoid Jeffrey Mayer's advice to minimise telephone discussions by telling the callers that: (a) you are in the process of leaving and only have a minute to spare; (b) you have someone in your office and would not want to keep him or her waiting; and/or (c) you have got a long- distance call on another line.[79] There are honest and virtuous ways in which one can shorten telephone discussions, such as by strictly limiting the discussions to business issues at hand, or telling the caller that you are not interested in his or her business and would, therefore, not want to engage in any further discussion about it.

4)   UNPRODUCTIVE MEETINGS.   Unnecessary and poor meetings are generally a time waster. Unnecessary meetings often stem from failure on the part of those convening them to determine whether or not they are the proper means for dealing with business issues at hand. Poor meetings, on the other hand, are a result of lack of concise agenda, poor chairmanship, unrealistic time limits, poor preparation, and so forth.

To be productive, meetings should meet the following conditions, among a host of other requirements: (a) they should be the appropriate vehicle for the business being addressed (in other words, they should be used only after determining that the business at hand can not be handled in any other way); (b) the goals or expectations they are expected to fulfil should be clearly stated in order to guard against aimless and superfluous discussions; (c) they should be convened with concise agenda, which should be followed strictly during deliberations to avoid going astray; (d) they should be started promptly at stipulated times, and they should be ended promptly without any undue delays; and (e) they should be presided over by people who are competent in terms of both team-building abilities and experience in conducting meetings.

5) PROCRASTINATION. Putting off taking action until a future time can lead to a piling up of work. Unless there are unanticipated contravening circumstances, therefore, all work scheduled for any given day should be completed to clear the way for future tasks. Delegation of part of one's work to a subordinate, if any, can be an effective way of ensuring that work is not postponed until a future time.

The process of *delegation* involves four basic steps; these are: (a) determining the tasks that can be delegated without giving up one's responsibility and which a given subordinate or employee is capable of accomplishing; (b) assigning the tasks to the employee or subordinate; (c) giving the employee or subordinate the necessary authority and support for accomplishing the tasks; and (d) checking periodically on the progress being made by the employee or subordinate.[80]

6) UNCLEAR JOB DESCRIPTIONS. Unclear job descriptions, or the lack thereof, can be a time waster because they can, among other things, lead to duplication of effort, non-performance of stipulated tasks, and role confusion. For these reasons, managers should ensure that all their subordinates have clear job descriptions. This can be helpful in many ways. First, job holders will know clearly what is expected of them; this will enable them to plan their work better than when they are not sure about their specific responsibilities. Second, they will find it easier to determine whether or not their subordinates are doing the work for which they are responsible, and evaluate their performance accordingly. Third, incidents of employees getting into each other's way, so to speak, will be reduced, or even eliminated, since they will know their specific responsibilities.

7) OTHER TIME WASTERS. There are also other factors which can lead to unwise or unproductive use of time in organisational settings, such as high employee attrition, poorly maintained machinery and equipment, and poorly designed facilities. The first factor, that is, high employee attrition resulting from regular resignations and/or involuntary terminations, can lead to time wasting in a number of ways; first, it can result in non-availability of adequate personnel to complete planned work on schedule. Also, a great deal of the time needed for task performance is usually spent on orientation and training of new hires. Moreover, new hires will often be relatively less efficient in

performing work assignments.

Poor maintenance of machinery and equipment can lead to regular breakdowns in a business's pieces of machinery and equipment and adversely affect employees' ability to cope with the demands of their work. And poorly designed facilities, such as those where the stockroom for merchandise or raw material regularly used by employees is awkwardly located, can be very costly in terms of the time wasted by employees to access raw materials or pieces of merchandise.

It is, therefore, essential for business executives to deal effectively with these time wasters by taking the following measures, among others: (a) initiating an incentive scheme designed to facilitate the retention of competent personnel; (b) ensuring that maintenance of machinery and equipment is done on a regular basis; and (c) consideration of operational efficiency in the design of business premises and facilities. With respect to the need for a scheme designed to retain competent employees, Whiteman-Jones has advised managers to seriously consider how much time and energy they spend on hiring, firing, and dealing with poor performance and conflicts in work schedules, as well as what they can accomplish with the time that can be "saved" by having a stable work force.[81]

## 5.3 MINDING ONE'S HEALTH

The health of any given executive is a critical element in his or her success in performing managerial tasks. It is, therefore, essential for executives to seek to enhance their managerial aptitudes and simultaneously strive to stay healthy, otherwise they should not expect to function effectively in their managerial careers. Suggestively, a programme to keep oneself healthy should include the following: regular physical exercises, regulated consumption of food and drink, regular medical check-ups, constructive relaxation, and adequate sleep.[82]

PHYSICAL EXERCISE. As most physicians would generally emphasise, exercise is very important to good health. There are many benefits that accrue from taking regular physical exercise. First, it can reduce the risk of contracting heart disease. Second, it can greatly help prevent rheumatic ailments such as lumbago, sciatica and fibrosis. Third, management specialists will usually advise that one takes physical exercise as a remedy for tension and an antidote for stress. Further, exercise provides increased stamina, mental alertness, and an enhanced feeling of well-being.

PROPER NUTRITION. A regulated course of food and drink, especially one prescribed by a dietician, can greatly contribute to an executive's health and vigour. There is no doubt that careless consumption of food and drink can, among other things, cause diarrhoea, constipation, and/or obesity.

MEDICAL CHECK-UPS. It is incumbent upon every manager to arrange to have regular medical check-ups. It is possible for some infectious diseases to be in one's body without showing any symptoms for some time. By the time symptoms begin to show, the infection may already be in an acute stage. A medical check-up can trace any such infections from one's blood, urine, or stool. This can make it possible for treatment to be administered before the infections can become a menace to one's health and vigour.

RELAXATION. When there are a few leisure moments, it is wise to use them to relax oneself. Spare time should be used to pursue a leisure activity that can fulfill one's potential, such as discussing business with friends over a light drink, watching a football or soccer match, taking an evening stroll, and the like.

ADEQUATE SLEEP. As much as possible, business executives need to allow themselves adequate sleep; it should be obvious that an executive who spends much of his or her nights drinking, rambling, or engaging in some other unconstructive activities cannot wake up in the morning with an alert mind and stance to undertake managerial pursuits and endeavours.

<>

# 6/ RETHINKING WESTERN MANAGEMENT

Historically, Western management theories, systems and practices have been regarded as the *sine qua non* in the efficient and effective management of both people and organisations. The emergence of Japanese management systems and practices, as well as their success in facilitating Japan's stunning accomplishments in both commerce and industry, has evoked a great deal of curiosity and interest among scholars and researchers. For modern Western executives, the emergence of Japanese management systems and practices is a reality which beckons them to re-examine their modes and systems of management.

The purpose of this chapter is to contrast salient Japanese and Western management views, attitudes and practices in an effort to demonstrate the fact that Japanese modes and systems of management pose a very significant challenge to Western modes and systems of management. Specifically, the following themes constitute the corpus of the chapter: important differences between Japanese and Western modes and systems of management, sources of these differences, and implications of the differences for business executives.

It should be noted here that, due to subtle differences in modes and systems of management among Western countries, only one Western country - the United States - is compared with Japan in the discussion both for reasons of simplicity and due to the fact that

Japanese modes and systems of management have been relatively more extensively studied in relation to those commonly used in the United States.

6.1 JAPANESE VERSUS WESTERN MANAGEMENT

There are many important differences between Japanese and American business and management systems and practices; among the more salient of these differences pertain to the following matters: industrial organisation, decision making, human resource management, and approach to customer satisfaction. A survey of each of these general areas of differences constitutes the corpus of the remainder of this section.

INDUSTRIAL ORGANISATION

Industrial organisation in Japan and the United States differs in terms of market structure and government-industry relationships. In the United States, the manner in which industries are organised is greatly influenced by antitrust legislation; moreover, a commitment to honour the ideals of *laissez faire* has resulted in the business community and the government being removed from each other. In Japan, on the other hand, antitrust legislation is non-existent and, in fact, the government actively sanctions and promotes collusion and monopoly; this is the basic reason for the existence of *zaibatsus* and *keiresus* in the country. Further, there is very strong government-industry cooperation; in fact, the business community looks upon the government as "a source of guidance and support."[83]

It is, therefore, important to note the fact that American-type industrial organisation, based as it is on government-fostered competition and the formal government-industry separation, cannot be successfully transferred to the Japanese society, where industrial organisation is deeply rooted in the country's culture, as Alan Goldman has implied in the ensuing excerpt:

> To attempt a break up of the Japanese corporate conglomerates is to 'mess' with many indigenous

> *culturally based social and business practices, built*
> *upon extremely close interrelationships, reciprocity,*
> *and mutual obligations and indebtedness.*[84]

In short, Japanese industrial organisation is an outgrowth of centuries of collectivism, which cannot easily give way to the *laissez faire*-based, American-style industrial organisation.

By and large, Japanese decision-making systems are participative in nature and are, therefore, generally different from the typically authoritarian mode of decision making commonly used in American business organisations; a good example is the "ringi" decision-making system, which is described in a nutshell in Chapter 3 of this book. Quality circles, also discussed briefly in Chapter 3, provide another good example. Theory Z management, too, serves to exemplify the participative nature of Japanese modes of decision making in organisational settings.

Quality circles, the "ringi" decision-making system, and Theory Z management are successfully used in Japanese organisations largely because of the unique values and traditions of Japanese society. The country's Confucianist doctrine of human respectability, coupled with a belief in the potential of individuals, naturally culminates in the design of work environments where managers spontaneously embrace, to use McGregor's work,[85] Theory Y assumptions about people.

In sharp contrast, the Judeo-Christian heritage of the United States (which emphasises human weaknesses and limitations) and the persistent legacy of Frederick Taylor's scientific management[86] have generally continued to breed Theory X managers in the country. In terms of Geert Hofstede's dimensions of national culture,[87] the differences in Japanese and American management systems and practices can be explained by means of the individualism-collectivism dimension. The participative kind of decision making in Japanese management can be said to be a result of the collectivist nature of Japanese society, while the authoritarian nature of American management can be attributed largely to the individualistic posture of American society.

Clearly, these deep-rooted differences between the two countries make it difficult for Japanese decision-making systems to be transferred to American institutions. There should, however, be no doubt that Americans can learn and practise Japanese decision-making approaches; in fact, the Japanese' apparent eagerness "to transfer management practices and expertise from [their country] ... to other parts of the world"[88] can greatly facilitate the re-orientation of American managers to the Japanese orthodoxy. This, of course, is not to suggest that it is possible for Western converts to have a complete change of outlook because, as an anonymous Indian maxim portends, "You can take an elephant out of the jungle, but you can never take the jungle out of an elephant." However, there is no telling how far the assimilation of the Japanese way of doing things can take the curious, open-minded and pragmatic Western executive.

To sum up, consensual or participative decision making and open communication are critical elements in Japanese management. Important decisions in Japanese institutions are, as such, generated by means of group interaction and cooperation through decision-making systems like quality circles, Theory Z management, and the "ringi" system - what one may label or characterise as "management by consensus."[89] In the United States, decision making, including problem solving, are generally the preserve of individuals.

HUMAN RESOURCE MANAGEMENT

There are many important differences in the manner in which the human resource is managed in Japan and the United States. In Japanese institutions, the human resource management function is both more extensive and more important than in the United States - a difference which is perhaps to be expected considering the fact that the function in the typical Japanese company regards employees as "life-long members of the corporate family"[90] and treats them as such through what is referred to as *kaizen*. In the remainder of this section, a contrast is made between Japanese and American staffing practices with respect to the following aspects of the staffing function: employee selection, employee remuneration, appraisals and promotion, training and development, career development, and labour-management relations.

EMPLOYEE SELECTION. Japanese companies generally prefer to hire young school graduates with little or no job skills, and then provide them with the necessary on-the-job training to prepare them for life-long employment - and this is precisely the basic reason why Japanese workers, as Susan Dentzer has noted, often refer to their employer-organisations as *uchi*, which means "home."[91] American companies, on the contrary, generally seek to engage externally trained job seekers partly to avoid the costs associated with on-the-job training.

REMUNERATION. There are several significant differences between Japan and the United States with respect to employee compensation and rewards; they include the following:

1) While the level and composition of remuneration are major factors for American job seekers, the size and reputation of an organisation are more important to their Japanese counterparts;

2) Union bargaining power has a greater influence on the level and composition of compensation in the United States than in Japan;

3) Individual employees are more seriously considered in the determination of rates of pay in Japan than in the United States;

4) Seniority and age are given greater consideration in the determination of pay rates in Japan than in the United States; and

5) Salaries and wages are generally based on age and seniority in Japan, and on performance in the United States, and are in general relatively lower in Japan than in the United States.

APPRAISALS AND PROMOTIONS. Both performance evaluations and promotions are slow and gradual in Japanese organisations, while in the United States there is pressure for quick evaluations and promotions. Moreover, promotions are based on age and seniority in Japan, and on performance (or merit) in the United States. These are apparently the most distinct differences between American and Japanese performance evaluations and promotions; other aspects of employee performance evaluations and promotions (such as the criteria, purposes and procedures pertaining to employee appraisals) have a lot in common.

TRAINING AND DEVELOPMENT. Training and development systems in Japan are designed to encourage individuals to acquire a variety of job skills through a relatively greater use of on-the-job and in-house training, while those in the United States emphasise specialisation in specific job skills.

CAREER DEVELOPMENT. In the United States, career development is designed to provide specialised career paths consistent with the needs and requirements of an employer; in Japan, on the other hand, it is designed to provide flexible, non-specialised career paths consistent with the development of each individual's life-time relationship with a given employer.

LABOUR-MANAGEMENT RELATIONS. Labour unions in Japan may be descri- bed as "enterprise unions" since they organise employees of single institutions. This and the fact that both blue-collar and white-collar personnel are enrolled in unions makes the unions and their organisati- ons' managements more of allies than adversaries. This differs radically from American labour unions, which are organised according to trades or industries, and enroll blue-collar employees to the exclusion of white-collar personnel. In terms of labour-management relations, Japanese companies have a close, cooperative relationship with labour unions; this is in sharp contrast to the generally ad- versarial kind of labour-management relations that exist in the United States.

CUSTOMER SATISFACTION

Japanese companies place relatively more emphasis on *quality* in an effort to provide greater value to their customers than American companies. According to Peter Drucker, Japanese enterprises have, in their quest to improve quality, shifted their attention "from total quality management toward zero-defects management" through delibe- rate "control of brain power."[92] And, as Masaaki Imai has pointed out, the responsibility for maintaining quality in Japan falls directly under the aegis of line managers, unlike in the West where quality is generally regarded as the quality control manager's responsibility "as if it is an entirely separate issue in management."[93] This heightened Japanese concern for quality has certainly served the customer well through access to relatively better and more durable, and yet lower-priced, products.

The two cultures - that is, American culture (generally characterised by individualism) and Japanese culture (a reflection of communitarianism) - also conceive of *customer service* in different ways; the former is driven by self-interest, and its guiding "principle" in business matters may, as such, be represented by the following statement: "Concentrate on your own self-interest, and you will automatically serve your customers and society better, which will in turn let you concentrate on your own self-interest."[94] Japanese culture, on the contrary, is characterised by selflessness, and the golden rule to be observed in business dealings in such a culture may be typified by the following proposition: "Serve your customers and society to the best of your ability, and you will automatically achieve your personal goals, which in turn will let you serve your customers and society to the best of your ability."[95]

## 6.2 SOURCES OF DIFFERENCES

There are several contrasting values between the American and Japanese cultures which account for the different ways in which managers in the two countries manage organisations and human resources; Arthur Whitehill has pinpointed the more important of these values. They are: kinship, loyalty, status-based relations, contractual relations, and bureaucracy. A delineation of the differences between the two countries' cultures with respect to each of these values follows.[96]

KINSHIP. Organisational life in Japan is, to reiterate, characterised by close, personal, and family-type relationships, which essentially reflect the importance Japanese people attach to kinship and the extended family. In the United States, on the other hand, belief in the nuclear family is reflected in individualism and self-interest.

LOYALTY. While interpersonal obligations are an essential component of both personal life and work life among Japanese people, they are generally peripheral to Americans.

STATUS. In contrast to Americans who have more concern for status symbols (such as reserved parking, corner offices, and carpeted offices), the Japanese are more concerned about the actual ranks they hold in either social or organisational settings.

CONTRACTS. The United States has a low-context culture, which clearly accounts for the prominence of legal action, explicit contracts, and the legal profession in the country. In contrast, the high-context culture of Japanese society is reflected in the very conspicuous distaste for formal, written contracts among the country's citizens.

BUREAUCRACY. Among the values considered, bureaucracy is apparently the only one which is common to both American and Japanese institutions. This is perhaps to be expected considering the fact that all large, complex institutions need to have a formal organisation structure, administrative procedures, and rules and regulations if they are to be viable.

## 6.3 IMPLICATION OF THE DIFFERENCES

The success of Japanese business and management systems and practices clearly signals the need for a re-examination of the efficacy and appropriateness of the Western *modus operandi* in managing the affairs and resources of an organisation, particularly in the 21st century. Unless they change their systems and modes of management, therefore, Western executives should not wonder when the overall productivity and competitiveness of their organisations decline remarkably and eventually turn them into third-rate participants in the global marketplace in the 21st century.

The unpleasantness of this potential state of affairs makes the following expressed desire of pundit Edward Lawler III (of the University of Southern California business school) the apparent and collective will of Western managers and their organisations:

*In the 1990s, we will reinvent management - and constantly modify our invention ... partly because the traditional systems of managing are failing.*[97]

# Appendix/
# Cultural Risk in
# Cross-Border Business

Today, more than ever before, more and more organisations are finding it inevitable to expand their operations beyond domestic markets; the motivations for such expansion include a desire for global leadership, the need to gain economies of scale and scope, the need for risk diversification, the quest for a higher return on investment, a desire for market expansion, and/or the quest for enhanced profitability. However, expansion of business operations across national borders exposes organisations to political, economic, and cultural risks. Let us briefly discuss the nature of these three classes of business risks.

The first, that is, *political risk*, may be viewed essentially as those governmental or societal actions and policies in a foreign country or region which are likely to thwart profitable business operations in such a country or region. The following are some of the important indicators of political risk which cross-border business operators need to look for: (a) government breaches, or unilateral revision, of contracts with foreign parties; (b) nationalisation and/or expropriation of foreign assets; (c) unreasonably strict restrictions on profit repatriation; and (d) default or repudiation of external debts by the government.

The second form of risk, that is, *economic risk*, pertains to unfavourable market conditions obtaining in a would-be host nation or region; such conditions may include the following: (a) inflationary trends; (b) deflations, depressions, or recessions; (c) unstable currency; (d) high tariffs and restrictive quotas; and (e) unstable industrial relations. *Cultural risk*, on the other hand, is the potential business risk which may emanate from serious inconsistencies or clashes between a transnational business's product offerings, or any other element of its operations, and the deep-rooted customs, values, beliefs, and/or attitudes of indigenous people in a given host country or region. The customs, values, beliefs, and/or attitudes alluded to here are among important elements of *culture*, a term which may be defined to refer to an integrated system of learned and shared behavioural patterns that are distinguishing characteristics of the members of a given tribe, country, or region.[98]

The remainder of this appendix is devoted to a survey of "cultural risk," particularly because it is a new concept; the other two (that is, political risk and economic risk) are widely discussed in most international marketing and international business books. First, a method for determining cultural risk is presented and, second, suggestions are made on how managers can use cultural risk scores to improve their chances of success in cross-border business operations.[99]

A.1/ MEASURING CULTURAL RISK

Cultural risk is, in this book, operationalised along two elements or dimensions of culture, that is, *language* and *religion*. The first element, that is, "language," is important in the determination of cultural risk because it is likely to create costly misunderstandings about a transnational company's sales promotion campaigns, public relations efforts, and the like. Poor or carelessly translated advertising statements, for example, can convey unintended messages which, from the point of view of customers in a foreign target market, may turn out to be "obscene, offensive, or just plain ridiculous."[100]

Besides, the existence of a diversity of languages in a country or region generally signals the presence of different tribal, ethnic, and/or other groupings of people with distinct customs and traditions which can be significant sources of conflicting attitudes and perceptions about work, products, and so forth, among the country's or region's people. In more general terms, as Robert Graham has postulated, "language can affect and even control the world view of its speakers."[101]

The other important dimension in the determination of cultural risk is "religion," whose importance arises from its potential to evoke moral-related and other issues and problems for a business and its goals, policies, and product offerings. This potential emanates from the overwhelmingly profound influence which religion has on people's habits, their outlook on life, the products they buy, the literature they read, the radio programmes they listen to, and the television programmes they watch. And, after all, one does not have to be a Salman Rushdie[102] to be able to figure out how strongly religious folk can safeguard, and are both influenced and guided by, their consecrated beliefs and practices.

Language and religion are useful in developing a "cultural difference" continuum, which can be used in forecasting the potential cultural risk in any given country or region.[103] Therefore, the necessary information needed here pertains to the different languages and religious denominations or groupings in the nation or region being considered for investment. Cultural difference is directly related to cultural risk in the sense that it has the potential to create tensions and misunderstandings between cultural groups and foreign business institutions in culturally different host countries or regions. The following excerpts should testify to this fact:

> *McDonald's has been invited to India - but told not to bring its Big Mac [beef burger]. To sell beef in the land of the sacred cow requires a special licence that is granted only to luxury-class hotels catering to foreign tourists. Beef [consumption] is taboo to Hindus, who are 82% of India's 875 million people. Moslems, who are 12% and the country's largest minority, don't eat pork.[104] And*

> *When Pepsi Cola decided to launch its products on the Israeli market ... it did not imagine that it would face rabbinical censure for challenging the biblical version of the origins of man. Although [it] ... has successfully sold Pepsi and 7-Up to atheists in Russia and Muslim fundamentalists in South Arabia, its apparently innocent appeal to new consumers in*

*[Israel] ... was described as [being] "blasphemous...."
The cause of the furor were newspaper and billboard
pictures depicting the first phase of Charles Darwin's
evolution of man, beginning with an ape ten million
years ago.*[105]

And "language," as an element of culture, can be measured by the
diversity of tongues spoken in a given country or region, while
"religion" can be measured by the diversity of religious groupings or
denominations in such a country. The specific steps involved in the
determination of the potential cultural risk associated with doing
business in a single foreign country and that associated with undertaking business operations in an economically integrated region (that is,
a free trade area, a customs union, a common market, an economic
union, or a monetary union) are outlined separately below.

THE COUNTRY LEVEL. Business managers may determine the cultural
risk associated with conducting business in any given foreign country
in several steps as follows:

1) Determining the total number of officially recognised languages in
the foreign country that are not common to those in the home country
(disregarding the languages in the home country which are not in the
foreign country), and then circling the language score associated with
this number in Figure A1;[106]

2) Determining the total number of religious groupings or denominations in the foreign country that are not common to those in the home
country (disregarding the religious groupings in the home country
which are not in the foreign country), and then circling the religion
score associated with this number in Figure A1;[107]

3) Adding the circled language and religion scores as follows:

$$C_i = L_i + R_i,$$

where

$C_i$ = cultural risk in country $i$, $L_i$ = language score for country $i$, and $R_i$ = religion score for country $i$; and

4) Plotting the result obtained in the preceding step on the cultural risk continuum in Figure A2 and, designating it as $C_i$ (that is, cultural risk in country $i$), interpreting the results as stipulated in Table A1 below.

THE REGIONAL LEVEL. If an executive wishes to determine the potential cultural risk associated with conducting business in an economically integrated region (such as the European Union, the Economic Community of West African States, or the Southern African Development Community) with a standardised marketing mix, he or she can do so in three steps as follows:

1) Calculating the cultural risk for each of the countries (that is, countries $C_1$, $C_2$, ... $C_n$) in the region using steps 1 through 3 outlined earlier;

Figure A1: Language/Religion Scores

| Uncommon lang-uages/religions | Language score | Religion score |
|---|---|---|
| 0 | +5 | +5 |
| 1 | +4 | +4 |
| 2 | +3 | +3 |
| 3 | +2 | +2 |
| 4 | +1 | +1 |
| 5 | 0 | 0 |
| 6 | -1 | -1 |
| 7 | -2 | -2 |
| 8 | -3 | -3 |
| 9 | -4 | -4 |
| $\geq 10$ | -5 | -5 |

2) Adding the cultural risk values calculated in step 1 for countries $C_1$ through $C_n$ and dividing the result by the number of countries in the region, N, thus:

$$\frac{C_1 + C_2 + \ldots + C_n}{N} \; ; \quad \text{and}$$

3) Plotting the result obtained in the preceding step on the cultural risk continuum depicted in Figure A2 and, designating it as $G_i$ (that is, the potential cultural risk in region $i$), interpreting the results as stipulated in Table A1.

## A.2/ USING CULTURAL RISK SCORES

Cultural risk scores can aid a business executive in figuring out whether or not much effort needs to be expended on adapting his or her organisation's policies, operations, and marketing mix to the idiosyncrasies of the cultural environment of a particular foreign target market. Therefore, the need to understand and manage cultural risk is an imperative which both practising and prospective managers of cross-border businesses should consider if they are to respond effectively to culture-related needs, challenges, and opportunities.

Table A1:  Interpreting Cultural Risk Results

| | |
|---|---|
| 1.  $10 \geq Z_i > 4$ : | low cultural risk. |
| 2.  $-4 \leq Z_i \leq 4$ : | moderate cultural risk. |
| 3.  $-4 > Z_i \geq -10$: | high cultural risk. |

$[Z = C_i, \text{ or } G_i]$

The amount of effort executives may need to expend on adapting their organisations' policies, operations and marketing mix will be dictated largely by the cultural risk score relating to the foreign target market involved. Some rules of thumb are suggested in the ensuing paragraphs for scores reflecting low, moderate, and high cultural risk, the ranges of which are given in Table A1. In each of the three cases, $Z_i$ is used to represent the potential cultural risk associated with conducting business in either a country or an economically integrated region.

1) Low Cultural Risk. If the cultural risk score for a particular target market falls in the range $10 \geq Z_i > 4$, minimum effort and resources should be devoted to the adaptation of a transnational company's marketing mix to the target market's cultural environment. This implies, for example, that executives do not really need the input and services of seasoned local analysts and translators in making their organisations' operational and marketing mix decisions.

Figure A2: Cultural Risk Continuum

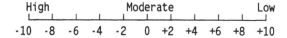

2) Moderate Cultural Risk. A cultural risk score falling in the range $-4 \leq Z_i \leq 4$ would require an executive to enlist the services of a couple of well-trained and experienced part-time local analysts and translators to help him or her in gaining a greater understanding of the cultural environment relating to the foreign target market. The analysts and translators can be regularly called upon to provide useful inputs and insights whenever management is formulating or reviewing the company's policies and/or marketing mix.

3) High Cultural Risk. Any given target market whose cultural risk score falls in the range $-4 > Z_i \geq -10$ would require a manager to hire, on a permanent basis, at least one local analyst or translator. The primary function of such an individual should be to work hand in hand with the responsible manager and other executives in adapting an organisation's policies, operations, and marketing strategy to the target market's cultural environment.

To underscore the necessity and importance of considering cultural and other related differences in cross-border business operations, one would perhaps do well to finally echo the following foreboding words of pundit Elliot Richardson:

> *For as far ahead as we can see, large-scale corporate success will rest in substantial measure upon ... [a] corporation's understanding of the long-term implications of its foreign activities, its ability to shape its program[me]s in conformity with intimate knowledge of local conditions, and the demonstration of a responsible approach to its new environment.*[108]

NOTES

1. Pritchett, P., *New Work Habits for a Radically Changing World* (Dallas, Texas: Pritchett and Associates, Inc., 1996), p. 6.

2. Kyambalesa, H., *Self-Employment: Secrets to Success* (Johannesburg, South Africa: Witwatersrand University Press, 1999), p. 3. [Forthcoming].

3. See Glueck, F.W., *Management* (Hinsdale, Illinois: The Dryden Press, 1980), pp. 67-68.

4. Pritchett, P., op. cit., p. 22.

5. For the original discourse on each of these six steps, see Kyambalesa, H., *Success in Managing a Small Business* (Brookfield, Vermont, USA: Ashgate Publishing Company, 1994), pp. 176-179.

6. Adapted from Thompson, A.A. and Strickland, A.J., *Strategic Management: Text and Cases* (Plano, Texas: Business Publications, Inc., 1984), p. 14.

7. In "problem diagnosis," it is important not to mistake the web for the spider, so to speak; often times, decision makers identify effects of existing problems as problems themselves and, as a result, they end up generating solutions that cannot effectively solve problems at hand.

8. Adapted from Hellriegel, D. and Slocum, J.W., *Management* (Reading, Massachusetts: Addison-Wesley Publishing Company, 1982), p. 350.

9. Hicks, H.G. and Gullet, R.C., *Modern Business Management: A Systems and Environmental Approach* (Auckland: McGraw-Hill Book Company, 1974), p. 193.

10. For a more detailed discussion, see Hellriegel, D. and Slocum, J.W., op. cit., p. 334.

11. See Bedeian, A.G., *Management* (Chicago: The Dryden Press, 1986), pp. 185-86 for a detailed discussion on conditions of certainty, risk and uncertainty.

12. Pappas, J.L. and Brigham, E.F., *Managerial Economics* (Hinsdale, Illinois: The Dryden Press, 1978), p. 83.

13. Hellriegel, D. and Slocum, J.W., op. cit., p. 20.

14. Adapted from Glueck, W.F., *Management* (Hinsdale, Illinois: The Dryden Press, 1980), pp. 669-93.

15. This concept, that is, "employee acquirement," was originally introduced in Kyambalesa, H., *Success in Managing a Small Business* (Aldershot, England: Avebury, 1994), pp. 182 and 183.

16. See Haynes, M.E., *Stepping Up to Supervisor*, Revised Edition (Menlo Park, CA: Crisp Publications, Inc., 1991), p. 83.

17. Renier, J., quoted in O'Toole, J., *Vanguard Management: Redesigning the Corporate Future* (New York: Berkley Books, 1985), p. 133.

18. See Blanchard, K. and Johnson, S., *The One Minute Manager* (New York: Berkley Publishing Group, 1982), p. 8.

19. All the personnel matters and issues cited here may seem to be adequately catered for in generally all organisational settings, but there are actually managers out there who overlook such matters and issues in spite of their awareness of potential legal implications for either slighting or flouting employees' rights in the work place.

20. Ephlin, D., "The Union's Role As Co-Manager," *Fortune*, March 26, 1990, p. 37.

21. Kilpatrick, J.J., "Poor Spelling Turns First Impression into Lasting Bad Impression," *Rocky Mountain News*, February 26, 1995, p. 114A.

22. For a survey of the requisite managerial skills alluded to here, see Kyambalesa, H., *Success in Managing a Small Business* (Aldershot, England: Avebury, 1994), pp. 159-173.

23. These two modes of decision making are to be contrasted with such popular modes as the following: management by exceptions (MBE), management by objectives (MBO), and management by walking around (MBWA).

24. The term "fax" is sometimes used to refer to either the written messages and/or pictures reproduced or the process by which the transmission of such messages and/or pictures is accomplished.

25. Some people use the term "mincing words" to refer to this variation of slurred speech.

26. Obviously, there is a need for an organisation's top management to create a climate that fosters open, two-way communication among organisational members if the efforts of communication senders and receivers are to achieve any meaningful results.

27. Kilpatrick, J.J., "Poor Spelling Turns First Impression into Lasting Bad Impression," *Rocky Mountain News*, February 26, 1995, p. 114A.

28. Pope, A., quoted in *New Webster's Dictionary of the English Language: Deluxe Encyclopaedic Edition* (United States of America: The Delair Publishing Company, Inc., 1981), p. BT-69.

29. Anonymous.

30. Organisational members sometimes engage in "lateral communications," which are not discussed in this book because they violate the management principle of "unity of command" and, as such, they are considered to be somewhat unorthodox in both theory and practice.

31. Note that these are "formal" communication efforts; communications that are informally transmitted to external parties by members of an organisation are not surveyed in this book.

32. Chase, A., "Advertisers Put Snake Oil in New Green Bottles," *The Denver Post*, July 14, 1991, p. 1H.

33. For a more detailed discussion of the customer relations function, see Section 4.1 of this book, and Kyambalesa, H., *Business Innovation and Competitiveness in the Developing World* (Aldershot, England: Avebury, 1993), pp. 36-46.

34. Excerpted and adapted from Kleiman, C., "It Pays to Keep Employees Happy," *The Denver Post*, November 6, 1994, p. 1J.

35. For a detailed theoretical presentation of the hierarchy of needs, see Maslow, A.H., *Motivation and Personality* (New York: Harper and Brothers Publishers, 1954), Chapter 5.

36. See McGregor, D., *The Human Side of Enterprise* (New York: McGraw-Hill Book Company, Inc., 1960), pp. 33-57; and Bennis, W.G. and Schein, E.H., eds., *Leadership and Motivation: Essays of Douglas McGregor* (Cambridge, Massachusetts: The Massachusetts Institute of Technology Press, 1966), pp. 5-7 and 15-20.

37. For definitions and discussions of these factors, as well as "content" factors, see Herzberg, F. et al., *The Motivation to Work*, Second Edition (New York: John Wiley and Sons Inc., 1959), Chapter 8.

38. See Vroom, V.H., *Work and Motivation* (New York: John Wiley and Sons, Inc., 1964), pp. 14-18.

39. See Adams, J.S., "Toward an Understanding of Equity," *Journal of Abnormal and Social Psychology*, November 1963, pp. 422-36.

40. See Ivancevich, J.M. and Matteson, M.T., *Organisational Behaviour and Management*, Second Edition (Homewood, Illinois: Richard D. Irwin, Inc., 1990), pp. 120-22.

41. To enhance the viability of quality circles and the other initiatives, executives also need to introduce a special incentive scheme designed to reward employees who may contribute useful ideas or innovations.

42. For an original exposition of this and other principles of management, see Fayol, H., *General and Industrial Management*, trans. Storrs, C. (London: Sir Isaac Pitman and Sons Limited, 1949), pp. 19-42.

43. Rapp, S. and Collins, T., *The Great Marketing Turnaround: The Age of the Individual - and How to Profit from It* (Englewood Cliffs, New Jersey: Prentice-Hall, Inc., 1990), p. 312.

44. Quoted in Kanter, R.M., *The Change Masters: Innovation and Entrepreneurship in the American Corporation* (New York: Simon and Schuster, Inc., 1983), p. 180.

45. The term "change" is used broadly here to refer to the deliberate adaptation of any element or aspect of an organisational entity (such as its policies, product offerings, technology, organisation structure, rules and regulations, work procedures, and the like) to existing or anticipated dictates of internal and/or external conditions.

46. See Silver, W.S. and Mitchell, T.R., "The Status Quo Tendency in Decision Making," *Organisational Dynamics*, Spring 1990, Volume 18/Number 4, pp. 34-46.

47. This conceptualisation of the change process was first introduced in Kyambalesa, H., *Success in Managing a Small Business* (Brookfield, USA: Ashgate Publishing Company, 1994), pp. 96-98.

48. See Herbert, T.T., *Dimensions of Organisational Behaviour* (New York: MacMillan Publishing Company, Inc., 1976), p. 361.

49. For an original discussion of these aspects of change, see Herbert, T.T., ibid., pp. 361-62.

50. Kouzes, J.M. and Posner, B.Z., *The Leadership Challenge: How to Get Extraordinary Things Done in Organisations* (San Francisco: Jossey-Bass Publishers, 1991), p. 77.

51. Toffler, A., quoted in Scott, C.D. and Jaffe, D.T., *Managing Change at Work: Leading People through Organisational Transitions*, Revised Edition (Menlo Park, California: Crisp Publications, Inc., 1995), p. 1.

52. Although this set of strategies is by no means a panacea for marketing problems, it can greatly enhance marketers' ability to deal successfully with many of the problems emanating from the turbulent socio-economic environment in which their marketing operations are undertaken.

53. Gaither, N., *Production and Operations Management: A Problem-Solving and Decision-Making Approach*, Fourth Edition (Chicago: The Dryden Press, 1990), p. 58.

54. "Customer relations" should not be confused with "public relations." While the former is a marketing function, the latter is essentially a corporate-level activity.

55. Pride, W.M. and Ferrell, O.C., *Marketing: Basic Concepts and Decisions* (Boston: Houghton Mifflin Company, 1977), pp. 102-103, and 105.

56. Davis, K. and Frederick, C.W., *Business and Society: Management, Public Policy, Ethics* (New York: McGraw-Hill Book Company, 1984), p. 300.

57. See Bagley, D.S. and Reese, E.J., *Beyond Selling: How to Maximise Your Personal Influence* (Cupertino, California: Meta Publications, 1987), p. 3.

58. The "Town Hall Meetings" are a semblance of the Japanese *ringi system* and *quality circles* discussed in a nutshell in Chapter 3; they have been used by some American companies in recent years in an effort to gauge employees' views and suggestions on how productivity can be enhanced.

59. Excerpted and adapted from Neuborne, E., "Fashioning a Revolution in Service," *USA Today*, March 29, 1996, p. 1B.

60. Excerpted from "Some of the Tough Talk from Akers' Outburst," *USA Today*, May 30, 1991, p. 2B.

61. For a complete listing of the questions alluded to, see Rapp, S. and Collins, T., *The Great Marketing Turnaround: The Age of the Individual -and How to Profit from It* (Englewood Cliffs, New Jersey: Prentice-Hall, Inc., 1990), pp. 310-311.

62. As explained elsewhere in this book, *public relations* should not be confused with *customer relations*; its basic role is to link the corporate entity with external parties, while the role of the customer relations function is to link an organisation's marketing unit and societal groups that constitute the organisation's clientele.

63. For a detailed discussion of the rights of shareholders, see Steckmest, F.W., *Corporate Performance: The Key to Public Trust* (New York: McGraw-Hill Book Company, 1982), pp. 177-181.

64. The information and data contained in an organisation's annual report should not include aspects that are likely to place the organisation at a competitive disadvantage.

65. Lee, G., "PR Firms Moving into Policing Quality of Foodstuffs," *The Sunday Denver Post* (Contemporary), July 14, 1991, p. 17.

66. Leahigh, A.K., "The History of 'Quote, Unquote' Public Relations," *Public Relations Quarterly*, Fall 1993 (Volume 38, Number 3), p. 24.

67. This case study is adapted from "Chloride Chief's Future Bleak," *Times of Zambia*, July 23, 1986, and Kyambalesa, H., *Business and Social Demands* (Lusaka, Zambia: ZPC Publications, 1990), pp. 30-31.

68. Centre for Behavioural Medicine, "Focus on Health: Worried? Irritable? Stressed?" *The Denver Post*, April 2, 1996, p. 10A.

69. Dart, B., "Stress Increasing Worldwide," *The Denver Post*, March 23, 1993, p. 2A.

70. See Dart, B., ibid.

71. See Adams, J.D., "A Variety of Ideas for Responding to Stress," in Adams, J.D., editor, *Understanding and Managing Stress: A Book of Readings* (San Diego: University Associates, Inc., 1980), p. 211.

72. See Bower, B., "Hopelessness Tied to Heart, Cancer Deaths," in *Science News*, Volume 149/Number 15, April 13, 1996, p. 230.

73. *Awake*, "Watching the World: Employee Burnout," August 8, 1993, p. 28.

74. Drawbaugh, C.C., *Time and Its Use: A Self-Management Guide for Teachers* (New York: Teachers College Press, 1984), p. 1.

75. McCay, J.T., *The Management of Time* (Englewood Cliffs, N.J.: Prentice-Hall, Inc., 1959), p. 6.

76. For a detailed discussion of each of these four benefits of using time wisely, see Mackenzie, A., *The Time Trap* (New York: American Management Association, 1990), pp. 14-25.

77. Henry Mintzberg has, however, portrayed the management task as involving the performance of interpersonal roles, informational roles, and decision-related roles. For a cursory look at these three sets of Mintzberg's managerial roles, see the end of Section 1.1 in the first chapter of this book.

78. Alexander, R., *Commonsense Time Management* (New York: American Management Association, 1992), p. 5.

79. See Mayer, J.J., *Time Management for Dummies* (Foster City, CA: IDG Books Worldwide, Inc., 1995), pp. 144 and 145.

80. Adapted from Koontz, H. and Weihrich, H., *Essentials of Management* (New York: McGraw-Hill Book Company, 1990), p. 187.

81. Whiteman-Jones, M., "Hiring and Keeping the Best: The 10 Commandments," *Colorado Business*, October 1993, p. 50.

82. Norfolk, D., "Keeping Fit to Manage," *Management Today*, February 1976, pp. 101-104.

83. Whitehill, A.M., *Japanese Management: Tradition and Transition* (London: Routledge, 1991), p. 92.

84. Goldman, A., *Doing Business with the Japanese: A Guide to Successful Communication, Management, and Diplomacy* (New York: State University of New York Press, 1994), p. 39.

85. McGregor, D., *The Human Side of Enterprise* (New York: McGraw-Hill Book Company, Inc., 1960).

86. Taylor, F.W., *Scientific Management* (New York: Harper and Brothers, 1947).

87. Hofstede, G., "Motivation, Leadership, and Organisation: Do American Theories Apply Abroad?" in Bartlett, C.A. and Ghoshal, S., *Transnational Management: Text, Cases, and Readings in Cross-Border Management* (Homewood, Illinois: Richard D. Irwin, 1992), pp. 252-71.

88. See Karatsu, H., *Tough Words for American Industry* (Cambridge, Massachusetts: Productivity Press, 1986), p. 139.

89. This concept was originally introduced in Kyambalesa, H., *Business Innovation and Competitiveness in the Developing World* (Aldershot, England: Avebury, 1993), p. 28.

90. See Whitehill, A.M., op. cit., p. 128.

91. Dentzer, S., "Downsizing: Will East Meet West?" *U.S. News and World Report*, December 11, 1995, p. 72.

92. Drucker, P.F., "Japan: New Strategies for a New Reality," *The Wall Street Journal*, October 2, 1991.

93. Imai, M., *Kaizen: The Key to Japan's Competitive Success* (New York: Random House, Inc., 1986), p. 203.

94. Extracted from a conceptual model presented in Hampden-Turner, C. and Trompennars, A., *The Cultures of Capitalism* (New York: Doubleday, 1993), p. 14.

95. Hampden-Turner, C. and Trompennars, A., ibid.

96. For an original analysis of these values, see Whitehill, A.M., *Japanese Management: Tradition and Transition* (London: Routledge, 1991), pp. 45-50.

97. Lawler III, E.E., "Let the Workers Make White-Knuckle Decisions," *Fortune*, March 26, 1990, p. 49.

98. Dahringer, L.D. and Muhlbacher, H., *International Marketing: A Global Perspective* (Reading, Massachusetts: Addison-Wesley Publishing Company, 1991), pp. 143-145.

99. Adapted from Kyambalesa, H., *Business Innovation and Competitiveness in the Developing World* (Aldershot, England: Avebury, 1993), pp. 8-18.

100. Frey, A.W. and Halterman, J.C., *Advertising* (New York: The Ronald Press Company, 1970), p. 563.

101. Graham, R.J., "The Role of Perception of Time in Consumer Research," *Journal of Consumer Research*, Volume 7, March 1981, p. 338.

102. The late Ayatollah Ruhollah Khomeini sentenced Salman Rushdie to death for authoring the novel entitled *The Satanic Verses* (New York: Viking Penguin, 1989), which the Iranian government considered to be blasphemous of the Islamic faith.

103. *Note*: "Language" and "Religion" are used in the determination of cultural risk in this book due to their being readily amenable to measurement.

104. "Golden Arches to Rise Beside Ganges: McDonald's to Leave Beef Behind in Appeal to the Indian Appetite," *Rocky Mountain News*, February 11, 1993.

105. Beeston, R., "Rabbis Froth Over Pepsi," *The Times* (London), May 15, 1992, p. 10.

106. Details pertaining to languages in various countries can be obtained from the following sources, among others: *Culturgram for the 1990s*, published in Provo, Utah, by Brigham Young University, David M. Kennedy Centre for

International Studies, Publications Services; *The World Almanac and Book of Facts* (which is published annually by Pharos Books, New York); Price Waterhouse publications on doing business in other countries; and area handbooks on various countries published by the U.S. Government Printing Office, Washington, D.C.

107. Information on religions in various countries can be obtained from the sources cited in the preceding endnote.

108. Richardson, E.L., "Introduction," in Ghadar, F. et al., editors, *Global Business Management in the 1990s* (Washington, D.C., Beacham Publishing, Inc., 1990), p. vii.

<><>

# GLOSSARY OF TERMS

*Accountability.* The final responsibility for results which a supervisor, an administrator, or a manager cannot delegate to anyone else in or outside his or her organisation.

*Administration.* The process or function of putting into effect the plans, policies, and/or rules and regulations generated by management in a given organisation or institution.

*Advertising.* A sponsored form of promotional communication transmitted through the mass media. Among the common forms of media that may be used for advertising are the following: the Internet, newspapers, rented billboards, signboards, television, magazines, journals, directories, catalogues, rented roadside benches, and the radio. Advertising is used by business organisations as well as individuals to promote such things as goods, services, programmes of study, political candidates, and ideas.

*Assets.* The things that a business owns, such as working capital, buildings, typewriters, vehicles, and machinery and equipment. For accounting purposes, assets are usually classified in two categories as follows:

a) *Current assets*: These include cash (both cash on hand and cash in the bank), accounts receivables, marketable securities, items that can be converted into cash within one year (such as inventories), and items that are normally used up in business operations within one year (such as materials and supplies); and

b) *Fixed assets*: A business's assets that cannot easily be converted into cash, such as land, buildings, vehicles, and machinery and equipment.

*Attrition.* See the term *employee attrition.*

*Authority.* The right to decide, to direct others to take action, or to perform certain duties in achieving stipulated organisational goals, including the right of decision and command over the allocation and application of available resources.

*Bait promotion.* A promotional method which involves the following, among other things: (a) inducing prospective customers to buy a product by asking them to test the product; (b) offering customers cash or quantity discounts; (c) promising them post-purchase services; and/or (d) offering customers credit facilities. Some organisations attempt to increase sales by sponsoring a contest which may involve pairing or matching coupons inserted inside bottle tops, packets of washing powder, and the like; buyers are enticed to buy more of the product involved in an attempt to find the pairing or matching coupons. This kind of sales-getting method is also a form of bait promotion. Another form of bait promotion involves placing attractive sales personnel (more especially ladies) at points of sale or service points.

*Balance sheet.* A statement that shows what a business owns and what it owes to various parties at a particular time period.

*Billboards.* Large boards mounted on poles along streets or highways, at beaches or parks, etc., on which advertisements are placed or affixed.

*Blue-collar employee.* Any of an organisation's production, maintenance, and service workers regardless of whether they are skilled, semi-skilled, or unskilled.

*Budget:* Any projection of revenues and expenditures prepared either by an organisation or by any of its operating units to serve as a tool for controlling the activities and operations of work groups and individual employees, supervisors, and managers in the organisation or operating unit.

*Bureaucracy.* A highly structured and centralised organisational system that is characterised by detailed and rigid administrative procedures and rules and regulations.

*Business.* (1) Any commercial or industrial undertaking created to engage in certain economic pursuits and endeavours with the major objective of making a profit. (2) Any activity or preoccupation in which a person or an organisation is involved over a considerable period of time, either for profit or for non-profit reasons.

*Business philosophy.* An organisation's written or unwritten principles that guide it in its business decision-making situations, as well as in its day-to-day operations.

*Business risks.* This term is used in this book to refer to the risks which an organisation which may decide to expand its operations beyond national borders may be exposed to; these are: *cultural risk, economic risk,* and *political risk.*

*Buyer.* (1) A customer. (2) A person engaged by an organisation to perform the function of procuring stationery, materials, and assets required by the organisation, among other things.

*Capital.* A business's total amount of money and/or property meant for use in ways that are intended to generate a return on the money and/or property.

*Career ladder:* A series of positions an employee is normally expected to move through up the hierarchy of an organisation and the minimum length of time he or she has to serve at each level. Synonymous terms used in organisational settings are *career path* and *career progression.*

*Change.* The deliberate adaptation of any element or aspect of a business entity (such as its policies, product offerings, technology, organisation structure, rules and regulations, work procedures, and the like) to existing or anticipated dictates of internal and/or external conditions.

*Common stock.* The type of shares of stock whose claims or rights on a corporation's earnings and assets come after those of *preferred stock.*

*Competition.* A market situation that exists when there are a large number of independent individuals or business undertakings producing and supplying similar products. While this situation is embraced by free market societies as necessary in fostering pronounced socio-economic development, it is usually attacked by socialist nations as being responsible for the "exploitation of man by man" in the world today. Also, socialist nations have attacked business competition for duplication of economic activities, which is considered to be wasteful of society's resources. It is, however, universally acknowledged today that business competition fosters economic efficiency and discipline and generally leads to a higher quality of life for the greatest number of people.

*Consumerism.* A social movement that seeks to augment the rights and powers of buyers in relation to those of producers and sellers. It is essentially a movement against unfair business practices, such as profiteering, or the making and selling of products of mediocre quality.

*Consumers.* A collection of buyers who purchase products for ultimate consumption, that is, for personal or domestic use. These constitute what are called *consumer markets.*

*Costing decisions.* Decisions concerning the following: determining marketing costs and setting prices (fees, charges, fares, rent, premiums, rates, interest, commissions, and the like) that will yield returns consistent with the overall goals of the organisation, while considering such factors as these. (a) customers' sensitivity to changes in prices; (b) costs of production; (c) prices of competing products, if any; and

(d) government pricing policy or regulations, if any. Traditionally, the term "pricing" has been used to refer to these and any other related decisions.

*Credit.* (1) A business favour extended to a customer to afford the customer the opportunity to have immediate access to a product or money in exchange for a promise of payment or repayment in the future. (2) An accounting entry on the liability side - that is, the right side - of an account, or the creation of (or addition to) an item of revenue or net worth. An entry designating either an increase in assets or a decrease in liabilities or net worth is referred to as a *debit.*

*Cultural risk.* The potential business risk which may emanate from serious inconsistencies or clashes between a transnational business's product offerings, or any other element of its operations, and the deep-rooted customs, values, beliefs, and/or attitudes of indigenous people in a given host country or region.

*Culture.* An integrated system of learned and commonly shared behavioural patterns, which distinguish one clan, tribe, or entire society from other similar groupings or collections of people. A culture may be said to be a "high-context" or "low-context" culture. A *low-context culture* is one in which verbal communication and expressions are more important than non-verbal communication and expressions, while the opposite is true for *high-context culture.*

*Currency.* (1) The money used in any given country, such as the Canadian dollar, the Zambian kwacha, the South African rand, the Indian rupee, the Japanese yen, and so forth. (2) Money that is in the form of bills and/or coins.

*Customer relations.* An organisation's planned effort aimed at creating and maintaining a positive interaction between the organisation and its customers, who are apparently among the most essential publics for any given business organisation. Essentially, customer relations is a deliberate effort at gathering and analysing information about the feelings and complaints of customers regarding an organisation's marketing mix - that is, its products, pricing/costing practices, promotional activities, and/or distribution system - and taking the necessary measures that will minimise any possible discontent among customers. Business organisations need to engage in customer relations for several reasons: (a) it is morally the right thing to do; (b) to gain reputation and protracted goodwill; (c) to ensure against loss of customers to existing and/or potential competitors; (d) to encourage the flow of information from customers, which can be useful in improving the organisation's marketing mix; and (e) to prevent any possibility of dissatisfied customers seeking legal action.

*Customers.* Buyers in general - that is, those who buy products for personal or domestic use as well as those who procure products for application in supporting or sustaining their business operations (such as manufacturers and re-sellers).

*Deflation.* A decrease in the general level of prices in an economy resulting from a reduction in the supply of money and credit.

*Delegation.* The process by which managers, administrators, or supervisors get work done through the efforts of others; it involves the following steps: (1) determination of tasks which can be delegated without giving up one's responsibilities, and which a given subordinate employee is capable of accomplishing successfully; (2) assigning of the tasks to the subordinate; (3) giving the subordinate the necessary authority, resources, and support for accomplishing the tasks; and (4) checking periodically on the progress being made by the subordinate.

*Demand.* The amount or quantity of a product that buyers are willing and able to buy in a given period of time at a given price.

*Depression.* A prolonged period in which business or economic activity in a country is at the lowest level, which is usually characterised by a high rate of business failures, little or no new capital investment, low incomes, mass unemployment, a decrease in credit, and so forth. A mild decline in a country's business activity is commonly referred to as a *recession*.

*Discount.* A deduction (made by a seller) from the original price of a product to benefit a customer who, for example, purchases a certain quantity of the product (*quantity discount*), or honours his or her debts within a particular period of time (*cash discount*), or procures the product for resell at a specified wholesale and/or retail price (*trade discount*).

*Distribution channel.* See the term *marketing channel.*

*Distribution decisions.* Decisions regarding storage, selection of distribution or marketing channels (that is, selling directly to product users or through agents, wholesalers and/or retailers) and transportation methods and facilities. Distribution decisions should be made systematically and simultaneously with the other marketing mix decisions (that is, product, costing, and promotion decisions) if the marketing effort is to yield any worthwhile results.

*Dividends.* Payments made to the owners of shares of stock as a return on their investment in a corporation.

*Economic risk.* This form of business risk pertains to unfavourable market conditions obtaining in a would-be host nation or region; such conditions may include the following: (a) inflationary trends; (b) deflations, depressions, or recessions; (c) unstable currency; (d) high tariffs and restrictive quotas; and (e) unstable industrial relations.

*Economy.* (1) Thrifty application or utilisation of material, financial, and other resources available to an organisation. (2) A state's or country's system of production, distribution, and consumption of products. (Note: A country's economy may be classified in several sectors as follows: (a) the *primary sector*, consisting of extractive activities like mining, agriculture, fishing, and forestry; (b) the *secondary sector*, composed of manufacturing, assembly, and processing firms; and (c) the *tertiary sector*, comprising such service-oriented activities as banking, insurance, tourism, and transportation).

*Emissary-style promotion.* A sales-getting tool used by some business organisations involving the deliberate use of their workers and managers to promote the organisations' products by using them (the products), as well as talking positively about them, during work and after-work situations.

*Employee attrition.* The gradual reduction in an organisation's work force resulting from employee retirements, resignations, and deaths.

*Equity Theory.* A theory which maintains that organisational members normally compare their individual performance and pay levels and those of other employees of equal standing, and that if they perceive an imbalance, they take such courses of action as the following, among others: (a) strive to get the imbalance removed by openly confronting their superiors; (b) deliberately reducing their level of performance; (c) engage in self-remuneration activities, such as pilfering; (d) decide to tolerate the imbalance; or (e) quit working for the organisation.

*Expectancy.* See the term *Expectancy model.*

*Expectancy Model.* A theory of motivation postulated by Victor Vroom, in which he theorised that an employee's motivation to work is a function of the following factors: (1) *expectancy* - the probability that one's effort can actually lead to the attainment of a stipulated performance target; (2) *instrumentality* - the probability that attainment of the stipulated performance target can lead to a particular reward, such as a promotion or a pay raise; and (3) *valency* - the value or importance a person attaches to the reward.

*Extensive exposure.* Popularisation of a product through wide exposure to prospective customers at public gatherings. This is done with the faith that it would attract more new customers and consequently result in greater sales volume. This method of promoting sales can be employed at such occasions as science, agricultural, and trade fairs. Also, religious congregations, sports gatherings, public meetings, concerts, and any other similar public occasions and rallies can be good media for popularising a product.

*Free market system.* A socio-economic system that is generally characterised by the following: (a) private ownership of property; (b) multi-party politics; and (c) a pluralistic social system.

*Fringe benefits.* Any form of compensation or reward given to an employee in addition to his or her wage or salary, such as paid vacations, a personal-to-holder car, medical insurance, long service bonus, and the like. Sometimes referred to as *perks*.

*Golden handcuffs.* Any form of fringe benefits granted by an organisation to an exceptionally skilled or talented employee that is intended to tie the employee to the organisation, such as a low-interest, long-term loan which the employee cannot easily pay back if he or she decided to leave the organisation for another job.

*Goods.* Tangible products (fully processed or otherwise) produced by agricultural, manufacturing, mining and construction companies.

*Goodwill.* The intangible value of a business organisation (quoted in monetary terms) gained through sound customer relations and public relations efforts, as well as through offering quality products, among other things.

*Grapevine.* The informal or unofficial channel of communication by which information is transmitted, usually from higher to lower levels of an organisation's hierarchy.

*Hierarchy of Needs.* This refers to the theory introduced by Abraham Maslow, which classifies human needs in ascending order as follows: (1) *physiological needs,* including the needs for food, water and shelter; (2) *security needs,* that is, the need for both physical and psychological safety and security; (3) *social needs,* including the needs for belonging, affection and affiliation; (4) *esteem needs,* such as the needs for respect, recognition and self-esteem; and (5) *self-actualisation needs,* including the needs for personal accomplishment and self-fulfillment.

*High-context culture.* See the term *culture.*

*Human resource management.* See the term *staffing.*

*Ideas.* Intangible products that are required to help in decision making and/or production operations. For example, ideas on how to operate a given machine, or how best to utilise one's time at work.

*Impulsive mail.* A sales-promoting tool involving the "scatter-mailing" of packages of information on, say, new product offerings, attractive price discounts, and/or professional services.

*Income statement.* A statement showing a business's sales and the various costs incurred during a specified period of time. Net income (or loss) is determined by subtracting the total costs incurred from the total sales attained during the period of time under consideration.

*"Infomercials".* A form of advertising whereby an organisation sponsors, say, a thirty-minute radio or television programme intended to demonstrate the uses and/or superiority of one or more of its products.

*In-house training.* A training programme arranged by an organisation for a selected number of employees, which may be conducted within or outside its premises by external experts, the general purpose of which is to provide an opportunity for employees to gain new knowledge and skills in specified fields so that they can be in a better position to respond effectively to technological, competitive, economic and other changes obtaining in the organisation's environment.

*Innovation.* The act or process of conceiving and/or tapping new ideas, and then implementing the more feasible of the ideas in an effort to improve the quality of an organisation's product offerings, minimise operational costs, and/or improve overall productivity.

*Instrumentality.* See the term *Expectancy Model.*

*Internet.* An electronic and computerised worldwide communications network.

*Investment.* (1) The commitment of one's money or property to the creation of goods and/or services with the ultimate objective of earning a return on the money or property. (2) The money or property employed by an individual or organisation in the creation of goods and/or services so that it can yield a return.

*Job description.* A set of statements concerning the nature, scope, and other pertinent aspects of any given job. The following are among important aspects which are normally included in job descriptions: job title, specific duties and responsibilities, immediate supervisor, and details stipulating the rights, privileges, salary scale, and fringe benefits attaching to the job.

*Job security.* The degree of stability and permanence of a person's current employment in a given organisation.

*Kaizen.* A Japanese term used to mean continued improvement in the quality of personal life, home life, social life, and working life.

*Keiresu.* The term used in Japan to refer to any group of enterprises (such as banks, suppliers, distributors, and retail outlets) that are linked together.

*Labelling.* An aspect of packaging which involves the following: (a) preparation of a slip of paper or plastic containing information about the producer or supplier, the contents, and so on; and (b) affixing or engraving the slip on the product, or on its container or wrapper.

*Low-context culture.* See the term *culture.*

*Management.* (1) The *group of persons* responsible for managing the affairs of an organisation. (2) The *discipline* concerned with understanding and improving the knowledge and skills in managing an organisation. (3) The *process* of coordinating and integrating the various resources of an organisation to accomplish specified targets and objectives.

*Management by consensus*: A concept used in this book to refer to the decision-making mode by which decisions on important matters are democratically made in formally constituted committees.

*Management by exceptions*. The mode of management which involves identifying cases of mediocre or unsatisfactory work performance and taking the necessary action that is likely to lead to the attainment of desired levels of performance. In other words, management by exception (MBE) is a management approach which focuses on behaviour or performance that is not consistent with organisational expectations.

*Management by objectives*. A systematic management approach which requires managers and administrators to focus on achievable goals in an effort to attain maximum results from financial, human, and other resources available to an organisation. Basically, the management by objectives (*MBO*) approach is accomplished as follows: (a) a superior and a subordinate first meet to discuss and jointly determine the goals to be pursued by the subordinate, the means or plan by which the goals are to be accomplished, and the manner in which goal-attainment is to be measured; and (b) the superior and the subordinate meet again to discuss both the subordinate's performance and issues or problems that need to be addressed to maintain or improve the attained level of performance.

*Management by rules*. Any decision-making or management style which emphasises the need for committees and/or individual decision makers to strictly adhere to stipulated decision rules or criteria in arriving at decisions on such matters as budget estimates, capital expenditures, hiring, pay levels, pay rises, promotions, demotions, transfers, dismissals, training, and granting of loans to employees.

*Management by walking around*. The mode or style of management whereby a manager or administrator visits his or her immediate subordinates' places of work on a regular basis to ask and answer questions about work-related issues and matters. The acronym of this style of management is *MBWA*.

*Market.* Any arrangement or mechanism for bringing sellers and buyers into contact with each other for the purpose of facilitating and expediting trade transactions. A market does not have to be a physical facility; buyers and sellers can get into contact with each other and get involved in commercial transactions by telephone, mail, the Internet, or any other possible means. Unofficial markets are commonly referred to as *black markets*, or *parallel markets*.

*Market share.* A percentage proportion of the target market secured by an organisation through its marketing programmes, while the remaining proportion is shared among competing organisations in the market. Factors that may help an organisation in gaining a larger market share include the quality of its product offerings, the appropriateness of its promotional campaigns, the level of its prices, and the efficiency of its distribution system. Essentially, market share reflects an organisation's actual sales against the market sales potential.

*Marketing.* A set of human activities involved in the creation, costing, promotion, and delivery of economic and/or social outputs that are intended to satisfy the needs and desires of existing and/or potential customers, users, audiences, or beneficiaries. The planning, organisation, implementation, and control of these activities is normally and appropriately referred to as *marketing management*.

*Marketing channel.* An organised network of independently owned agencies and institutions which, in collaboration, perform the activities that are necessary in linking a given supplier with buyers or users of products in order to accomplish the marketing task. Suppliers have several marketing or distribution channel alternatives: selling directly to product users or through agents, wholesalers, and/or retailers. The decision regarding which alternative to use will usually be influenced by such factors as the nature of the product involved and availability of marketing intermediaries.

*Marketing mix.* The composite of the following marketing variables or elements: (a) the product; (b) price; (c) promotion; and (d) distribution. These marketing mix elements are controllable to marketing managers in free enterprise economies. In state-controlled economic systems, however, marketing executives do not generally have full control over the management of these elements.

*Marketing strategy.* A comprehensive and integrated marketing plan designed to achieve stipulated marketing, and consequently organisational, objectives. It is a detailed description of the following: (a) the target market at which an organisation intends to direct its marketing efforts, and (b) the marketing mix designed to meet the specific needs and desires of the designated target market. Also referred to as a *marketing plan.*

*Middlemen.* Wholesalers, retailers, brokers, and any other independently owned agencies which may be used by a producer in distributing its products to industrial buyers and/or ultimate consumers. Also referred to as *marketing intermediaries.*

*Money.* Anything that is widely accepted as a *medium of exchange, unit of account, measure of value,* and/or *store of value* by creditors and sellers of products.

*Morale.* An employee's short-term and situation-specific preparedness (prompted by the presence of some action-evoking conditions or circumstances) to contribute positively toward the attainment of his or her employer-organisation's objectives.

*Motivation.* The process by which an employee's desire to work is energised, directed toward the accomplishment of stipulated goals, and sustained long enough for the goals to be attained.

*Need for affiltation.* A social need which drives or motivates a person to seek out individuals with whom he or she can associate.

*Need for belonging.* A social need which propels a person to seek to be treated and recognised as a worthy and needed member of a particular organisation, work unit, or work group.

*Negotiation.* The process by which two or more parties engage in discussions for the purpose of reaching a mutually satisfying business deal through an honest exchange of information.

*On-the-job training.* A method used by some organisations in enhancing the skills and productivity of new employees (especially trainees), which blends imparting knowledge related to a particular job with application of the knowledge to the actual job. Such training is normally conducted by people employed within an organisation, such as training officers and/or supervisors.

*Organisation chart.* A graphic portrayal or representation of an organisation's formal relationships of authority, responsibility, and accountability which organisational members are expected to observe in their day-to-day interactions at work.

*Organisation structure.* A framework which explains the nature and scope of the formal relationships of authority, responsibility, and accountability in an organisation. These relationships are usually graphically explained by means of organisation charts.

*Packaging.* The placing of products in containers or covering them with wrappers while providing for such aspects as economy, protection and convenience. In competitive economies, packaging should also include attributes that will add a promotional dimension to product offerings. But in monopolistic economies where there are hardly any alternatives to most products (particularly essential commodities), monopolistic suppliers do not find it necessary to provide for promotional considerations when making packaging decisions - the naked products (such as bread and bathing soap) and containers without labels testify to this fact.

*Personal selling.* This is usually cited as an element of the traditional promotional mix. But in the literal sense, the term is merely a convenient misnomer because it implies selling a product in person rather than through marketing intermediaries. For this reason, the term *sales talk* is preferred in this book and, therefore, replaces the term "personal selling."

*Peter Principle.* The principle holds that employees in organisational settings tend to rise to their levels of incompetence, implying that every job position in any given organisation tends to be held by a person who is incompetent to discharge its duties. See Peter, L.J. and Hull, R., *The Peter Principle: Why Things Always Go Wrong* (New York: William Morrow, 1969), p. 162.

*Physical distribution.* The storage and movement of products from producers to final users. Physical distribution decisions are generally those pertaining to warehousing, inventory handling and transportation methods as products change hands from the producer to the final user.

*Political risk.* This form of risk may be defined to include those governmental or societal actions and policies in a foreign country or region which are likely to thwart profitable business operations in such a country or region; the following are some of the important indicators of political risk which cross-border business operators need to look for: (a) government breaches, or unilateral revision, of contracts with foreign parties; (b) nationalisation and/or expropriation of foreign assets; (c) unreasonably strict restrictions on profit repatriation; and (d) default or repudiation of external debts by the government.

*Pollution.* Any form of contamination of the physical environment emanating from by-products and effects of industrial, commercial and other human activities.

*Preferred stock.* The type of shares of stock whose rights or claims on a corporation's earnings and assets come before those of common stock.

*Price.* The value (monetary or otherwise) placed on a product for exchange purposes. Many different terms are used for "price" in different exchanges, such as the following: fee, tuition, rent, fare, rate, interest, toll, premium, salary, wage, and tax. Price is commonly quoted in monetary terms. In barter trade, however, price is quoted in terms of how many units or weights of a product are required in exchange for another.

*Product.* A set of tangible and/or intangible attributes including functional, social, and psychological benefits that are derived from an exchange transaction. The term is broadly defined to include such things as ideas, services, goods, or graduates from educational institutions, or any combination of the four.

*Product decisions.* Decisions concerning the following: making changes to existing products, branding, packaging, adding new products to existing ones, phasing out unprofitable products, and so forth.

*Productivity.* The ratio or relationship between production inputs and outputs. The *inputs* include material, human, financial, and other resources employed in production processes. The *outputs*, on the other hand, are the tangible and/or intangible products that are created, that is, the results attained from production processes. Productivity is a central issue in the management of any and every business organisation; it is said to be high if increases in total outputs are greater than increases in total inputs, measured in monetary terms. For an organisation whose outputs are greater than the inputs used to produce the outputs, this may be expressed algebraically thus:

$$\frac{\text{Outputs}}{\text{Inputs}} > 1.$$

*Profit.* The amount of money an organisation gets over and above the cost of producing and/or selling a commodity. This is determined by subtracting the total costs incurred from the total revenue (total receipts or sales) realised. If the total cost is greater than the total receipts, an organisation incurs a loss.

*Promotion decisions.* Decisions concerning the following: determining the appropriate promotional mix of advertising, publicity, sales talk, bait promotion, shop garnishment, extensive exposure, customer relations, impulsive mail, and emissary-style promotion. In traditional marketing, the promotional mix comprises advertising, publicity, sales promotion, and personal selling.

*Psychogenic illness.* Any illness originating from, or relating to, the mind, such as dizziness, headaches, sleepiness, and nausea.

*Publicity.* A promotional tool that includes the following promotional activities: (a) point-of-sale posters and placards; (b) writings on product packaging, shirts, caps, vehicles, company-erected billboards and/or roadside benches, walls of buildings, and so on; and (c) positive information (not initiated or sponsored by the organisation) transmitted by news reporters and other parties about the organisation's products, prices, distribution system, and so on.

*Quality circles.* A Japanese management practice which provides for work groups to meet regularly - say, once every month - to critically discuss how their performance can be improved.

*Quantity discount.* A percentage deduction from the original price of a product made by a seller to benefit a customer based on the quantities bought by the customer. It may be a formal policy of the seller to effect deductions from the list price of a given product if a buyer's purchases are in excess of certain quantities.

*Quota.* A limit imposed by a country's government on the quantities of a given commodity that can be imported into the country (import quota), or exported out of the country (export quota).

*Rank and file.* The category of a business organisation's personnel who do not hold any supervisory, administrative, or managerial positions in the organisation.

*Raw materials.* Production inputs used in making final products; they include recycled solid wastes and extracts from mines, forests, farms, and the sea.

*Recession.* See the term *depression*.

*Refresher course.* A short training programme organised for the purpose of providing employees with an opportunity to review and update previously acquired job-related knowledge and skills.

*Repeat sales.* Continued and sustained buying of an organisation's products resulting from pronounced customer services and quality product offerings, among other things. Sustained customer patronage is the key to the survival of any and every manager. This is one reason why it is not advisable for executives to sell products of marginal quality or engage in practices that are likely to result in customer discontent, because such actions are bound to lead to a loss of customers to existing and/or potential competitors.

*Responsibility.* An obligation (on the part of an employee) to perform certain work activities or assignments.

*Retailers.* Small or large business undertakings that serve as middle-men or intermediaries between producers and consumers, or between wholesalers and consumers. They procure products from producers and/or wholesalers for the purpose of reselling them to final users.

*Ringi decision-making system.* A Japanese decision-making system in which an organisation encourages individual middle-level managers to generate or suggest innovative ideas and prepare a plan or proposal (referred to as a *ringisho*) on how the ideas can be implemented to the benefit of the organisation. The system may be described in a nutshell as follows: (a) the written proposal, or ringisho, is initially circulated among the sponsor's peers for examination and comments; and (b) if it is accepted (either as suggested by the sponsor or with some suggested modifications) by the sponsor's peers, the ringisho is finally sent to the organisation's top management for evaluation and possible approval.

*Salary.* The kind of remuneration that is paid weekly or monthly to clerical, executive, and professional personnel in an organisation.

*Sales promotion.* In traditional marketing literature, this is usually cited as a component of the promotional mix. In this book, however, the term is not preferred and is, therefore, not defined because it is misleading since the other elements of the promotional mix are forms of sales promotion, too.

*Sales talk.* A promotional tool employed by sales persons engaged in either customer-to-customer (personal) selling or selling in retail shops to arouse buyers' interest in a given product. Ordinarily, the sales talk should involve the provision of information about the advantages of a given product over other similar products and its unique attributes. Also, a product's price compared to those of competing products should be highlighted, especially if it is relatively lower. Other aspects that may be brought out in the sales talk may include the buyer's freedom to exchange a product bought for another, or seek reimbursement, if the product does not measure up to the claimed or expected quality or standard.

*Seminar.* (1) A short course arranged for a group of students or employees so that they can intensively study or discuss one or more selected topics under the tutelage of an instructor. (2) A gathering of people from a particular profession or vocation who have one or more subjects of common interest to discuss or study.

*Services.* (1) Intangible industrial products (such as banking services, legal services, labour, and insurance) required by organisations to provide other products. (2) Intangible consumer products such as shoe-shining, laundering services, and so forth. (3) Intangible products provided by municipal councils and the government, such as fire protection, police protection, sewerage services, health services, and other public services.

*Shareholder.* Any person, group of persons, or institution that owns shares of stock in a corporation. Also commonly referred to as *stockholder*.

*Shop garnishment.* A promotional method which involves improving the scenery at the point of sale. A number of things can be done, including the following: (a) installation of better and attractive shelving; (b) improving lighting and ventilation; (c) provision of soft piped music; (d) organisation of a shop into sections according to product groups; (e) installation of adequate buying points to prevent queues; (f) providing adequate and safe packing lots; (g) decorating walls; and (h) providing adequate and convenient shopping trolleys and baskets.

*Signboard.* A plastic, canvas or wooden placard displaying a promotional message sponsored by an organisation to boost the sales of its products, which may be affixed to, say, a shopping cart of a major retail store, the rear of a low-flying aircraft, or the interior or exterior of a mass-transit vehicle.

*Social responsibility.* An obligation for business owners and their enterprises to consider and minimise the negative impacts of their decisions and operations on customers and society at large.

*Span of control.* The number of subordinates who are under the direct supervision of any given manager, administrator, or supervisor. Sometimes referred to as *span of management.*

*Staffing.* The process or function whose purpose is to provide and retain competent human resources which an organisation needs to be able to bolster its operations. It involves the following: human resource planning, employee acquirement, remuneration, performance appraisals, maintenance of discipline among employees, and employee training and development. The process is also commonly referred to as *human resource management.*

*Stakeholders.* The various societal members (businesses, individuals, interest groups, and so forth) who are, or are likely to be, affected by an organisation's decisions, policies, programmes, and/or operations.

*Stress.* The mental, emotional, and/or physical strain or discomfort which an individual may experience due to such factors as the following: (a) unfavourable life experiences like death in one's family or a breakdown in one's valued social relationships, which may affect one's ability to cope with normal work demands; (b) personal incompetence or inability to perform the duties of one's job or position; and/or (c) organisation-based factors like work overload, interpersonal conflict, role ambiguity, and the like.

*Suppliers.* Organisations that provide such things as equipment, raw materials, services or merchandise to other organisations, or to individuals or households, for consumption or application in the production of products.

*Supply.* The quantity or amount of a product that suppliers are willing and able to offer for sale at a given price per time period. The term is normally used to refer to the amount or quantity of any given product offered for sale by producers, not marketing intermediaries.

*System.* Any set of interacting elements that share a common conceivable boundary separating the set of elements from other definable sets of elements. Examples of what may be regarded as a system include the human body, a clock, a car, a family, and a business organisation.

*Target market.* A group of customers for whom an organisation creates and maintains a marketing mix that is consistent with the specific needs and preferences of the customers in the group. An organisation's target market can be a segment of a given total market or the entire total market, where the total market may be a nation, a region, or the entire world.

*Tariff.* A tax or levy imposed by a country's government on goods entering or leaving the country - that is, on imports or exports. Normally used synonymously with the term *customs duty*. Tariffs, or customs duties, take several forms as follows: (a) *ad valorem tariff*: this is based on the monetary value of the commodity involved and is normally expressed as a percentage of the price of the commodity; (b) *specific tariff*: this type of tariff takes the form of a specified charge per unit, quantity or weight of a commodity; and (c) *compound tariff*: this is essentially a levy that consists of both an ad valorem and a specific tariff.

*Telemarketing.* An innovation in marketing which involves the use of telephones to access consumers.

*Theory X.* This represents a set of views or assumptions that portray human beings as being naturally lazy, disinterested in achievement, resentful of responsibility, and, among a host of other things, as lacking integrity. *Theory Y,* on the other hand, is a set of contrary views or assumptions about the nature of human beings.

*Theory Z.* A Japanese management philosophy that seeks to integrate life-time employment, consensual decision making, holistic concern for each and every employee, open communication, and the like, as ways and means of ensuring the long-term success and survival of an organisation.

*Training and development.* A formally instituted, organisation-wide programme designed to ensure that employees' knowledge and skills are continually improved and upgraded through seminars, workshops, refresher courses, on-the-job training, and in-house training. The ultimate purpose of such a programme is to reap the following benefits, among others, which are generally associated with having a sufficiently skilled work force: improved quality and quantity of product offerings, and a reduction in both waste and accidents at places of work.

*Two-Factor Theory.* This is a theory of motivation introduced by Frederick Herzberg. Essentially, the theory is explained in terms of the following two sets of factors: (1) "job content" factors, which are directly related to the job itself and are also sometimes referred to as *motivators* or *satisfiers*; and (2) "job context" factors, which are basically aspects that are peripheral to the job itself and are sometimes alternatively referred to as dissatisfiers, hygiene factors, or mainte-nance factors.

*Valence.* See the term *expectancy model.*

*Wage.* The hourly earnings of any given organisation's manual or menial workers.

*Warranty.* A written or verbal pledge made by a seller to a buyer of a product (especially in the case of technically complex products) indicating that, in the event of product failure not resulting from the buyer's fault, the concerned product would be replaced or repaired free of charge (or at a nominal charge) if the failure occurs before the expiry of a specified period of time. Such pledges are called "express" warranties. However, there are also "implied" warranties which are assumed from the fact that the mere selling of a product implies that the seller is giving an assurance to the buyer that the product will adequately serve the purpose for which it is intended.

*White-collar worker.* Any employee in an organisation whose work involves non-physical tasks or activities.

*Wholesalers.* Entrepreneurs or business undertakings that serve as independent middlemen or intermediaries between producers and retailers.

*Working conditions.* A package of information stipulating the rights, privileges, salary scale, fringe benefits, and other important details and provisions attaching to an employee while he or she is in the service of an organisation in a given position. Also referred to as *conditions of service.*

*Workshop.* A training programme organised to study or discuss a particular subject, the general purpose of which is to improve the knowledge and skills of participants through such pedagogical approaches as case analysis, group and individual presentations and exercises, and so on.

*Zaibatsu.* A Japanese term used to refer to any family-dominated group of business undertakings.

<>

# BIBLIOGRAPHY

Adams, J.D., editor, *Understanding and Managing Stress: A Book of Readings* (San Diego: University Associates, Inc., 1980).

Adams, J.S., "Toward an Understanding of Equity," *Journal of Abnormal and Social Psychology*, November 1963.

Alexander, R., *Commonsense Time Management* (New York: American Management Association, 1992).

American Assembly of Collegiate Schools of Business and the European Foundation for Management Development, *Management for the XXI Century: Education and Development* (London: Kluwer/Nijhoff Publishing, 1982).

Bagley, D.S. and Reese, E.J., *Beyond Selling: How to Maximise Your Personal Influence* (Cupertino, California: Meta Publications, 1987).

Baker, M.J., editor, *The Marketing Book* (London: W.M. Heinemann Limited, 1987).

Band, W.A., *Touchstones: Ten New Ideas Revolutionising Business* (New York: John Wiley and Sons, Inc., 1994).

Bartlett, C.A. and Ghoshal, S., *Transnational Management: Text, Cases, and Readings in Cross-Border Management* (Homewood, Illinois: Richard D. Irwin, Inc., 1992).

Basil, D.C., *Managerial Skills for Executive Action* (New York:

American Management Association, 1970).

Bennis, W.G. and Schein, E.H., editors, *Leadership and Motivation: Essays of Douglas McGregor* (Cambridge, Massachusetts: The Massachusetts Institute of Technology Press, 1966).

Berg, E.J., "Socialist Ideology and Marketing Policy in Africa" in Moyer, R. and Hollander, S.C., editors, *Markets and Marketing in Developing Economies* (Homewood, Illinois: Richard D. Irwin, Inc., 1968).

Bergin, J.F., *Practical Communication* (London: Pitman Publishing Limited, 1981).

Beveridge, A.A. and Oberschall, A.R., *African Businessmen and Development in Zambia* (Princeton, New Jersey: Princeton University Press, 1979).

Blanchard, K. and Johnson, S., *The One Minute Manager* (New York: Berkley Publishing Group, 1982).

Boje, D.M. and Dennehy, R.F., *Managing in the Postmodern World: America's Revolution Against Exploitation* (Dubuque, Iowa: Kendall/Hunt Publishing Company, 1993).

Bozeman, B., *Public Management and Policy Analysis* (New York: St. Martin's Press, 1979).

Cleveland, H., *The Future Executive: A Guide for Tomorrow's Managers* (New York: Harper and Row, 1972).

Committee on Definitions, *Marketing Definitions: A Glossary of Marketing Terms* (Chicago: American Marketing Association, 1960).

Dahringer, L.D. and Muhlbacher, H., *International Marketing: A Global Perspective* (Reading, Massachusetts: Addision-Wesley

Publishing Company, 1991).

Dalrymple, P.J. and Parsons, L.J., *Marketing Management: Text and Cases* (New York: John Wiley and Sons, 1980).

Davis, K. and Frederick, F.C., *Business and Society: Management, Public Policy, Ethics* (New York: McGraw-Hill Book Company, 1984).

Dentzer, S., "Downsizing: Will East Meet West?" *U.S. News and World Report*, December 11, 1995.

Douglass, M.E. and Douglass, D.N., *Manage Your Time, Manage Your Work, Manage Yourself* (New York: American Management Association, 1980).

Drawbaugh, C.C., *Time and Its Use: A Self-Management Guide for Teachers* (New York: Teachers College Press, 1984).

Drucker, P.F., "Consumerism: The Opportunity of Marketing," in Gaedeke, R.M. and Etcheson, W.W., editors, *Consumerism: Viewpoints from Business, Government, and the Public Interest* (San Francisco: Canfield Press, 1972).

_____ *Management: Tasks, Responsibilities, Practices* (New York: Harper and Row, 1973).

_____ "Marketing and Economic Development," Thorelli, H. and Becker, H., editors, *International Marketing Strategy* (New York: Pergamon Press, 1980).

_____ "Japan: New Strategies for a New Reality," *The Wall Street Journal*, October 2, 1991.

Dunlop, J.T., "The Social Utility of Collective Bargaining," in Ulman, L., editor, *Challenges to Collective Bargaining* (Englewood Cliffs, New Jersey: Prentice-Hall, 1967).

Dunning, J.H. and McQueen, M., "The Eclectic Theory of the Multinational Enterprise and the International Hotel Industry," in Rugman, A.M., editor, *New Theories of the Multinational Enterprise* (New York: St. Martin's Press, 1982).

Elliot, K. and Lawrence, P., *Introducing Management* (England: Penguin Books Limited, 1985).

Fayol, H., *Industrial and General Administration*, trans. Coubrough, J.A. (Geneva: International Management Institute, 1930).

_____ *General and Industrial Management*, trans. Storrs, C. (London: Sir Isaac Pitman and Sons Limited, 1949).

Fubara, A.B., "Marketing Planning in Public Enterprises in Developing Countries," *Zambia Journal of Business*, Volume 4/Numbers 1 and 2, April/August 1985.

Gaither, N., *Production and Operations Management: A Problem-Solving and Decision-Making Approach*, Fourth Edition (Chicago: The Dryden Press, 1990).

Ghadar, F. et al., editors, *Global Business Management in the 1990s* (Washington, D.C., Beacham Publishing, Inc., 1990).

Glueck, W.F., *Management* (Hinsdale, Illinois: The Dryden Press, 1980).

Goldman, A., *Doing Business with the Japanese: A Guide to Successful Communication, Management, and Diplomacy* (New York: State University of New York Press, 1994).

Graham, R.J., "The Role of Perception of Time in Consumer Research," *Journal of Consumer Research*, Volume 7, March 1981.

Halal, W.E., *The New Management: Democracy and Enterprise Are Transforming Organisations* (San Francisco: Berrett-Koehler

Publishers, 1996).

Hampden-Turner, C. and Trompennars, A., *The Cultures of Capitalism* (New York: Doubleday, 1993).

Harris, P.R. and Moran, R.T., *Managing Cultural Differences* (Houston: Gulf Publishing Company, 1982).

Hart, N.A., *Marketing of Industrial Products* (London: McGraw-Hill United Kingdom Limited, 1984).

Haynes, M.E., *Stepping Up to Supervisor*, Revised Edition (Menlo Park, CA: Crisp Publications, Inc., 1991).

Hellriegel, D. and Slocum, J.W., *Management* (Reading, Massachusetts: Addison-Wesley Publishing Company, 1982).

Herbert, T.T., *Dimensions of Organisational Behaviour* (New York: The McMillan Publishing Company, 1973).

Herzberg, F. et al., *The Motivation to Work*, Second Edition (New York: John Wiley and Sons Inc., 1959).

Herzberg, F., *Work and the Nature of Man* (Cleveland, Ohio: World Publishing Company, 1966).

Hofstede, G., "Motivation, Leadership, and Organisation: Do American Theories Apply Abroad?" in Bartlett, C.A. and Ghoshal, S., *Transnational Management: Text, Cases, and Readings in Cross-Border Management* (Homewood, Illinois: Richard D. Irwin, Inc., 1992).

Huseman, R.C. et al., *Business Communication: Strategies and Skills* (New York: CBS College Publications, 1985).

Imai, M., *Kaizen: The Key to Japan's Competitive Success* (New York: Random House, Inc., 1986).

Ivancevich, J.M. and Matteson, M.T., *Organisational Behaviour and Management*, Second Edition (Homewood, Illinois: Richard D. Irwin, Inc., 1990).

Karatsu, H., *Tough Words for American Industry* (Cambridge, Massachusetts: Productivity Press, 1986).

Kilpatrick, J.J., "Poor Spelling Turns First Impression into Lasting Bad Impression," *Rocky Mountain News*, February 26, 1995.

Koontz, H. and Weihrich, H., *Essentials of Management* (New York: McGraw-Hill Book Company, 1990).

Kotler, P., "What Consumerism Means to Marketeers," *Harvard Business Review*, May-June 1972.

_____ *Marketing Management: Analysis, Planning and Control* (London: Prentice-Hall International, 1984).

_____ *Marketing Management: Analysis, Planning, and Control* (Englewood Cliffs, New Jersey: Prentice-Hall, Inc., 1980).

Kurtz, D.L. and Boone, L.E., *Marketing* (New York: The Dryden Press, 1984).

Kyambalesa, H., *Business and Social Demands* (Lusaka, Zambia: Zambia Publishing Company Publications, 1990).

_____ "A Fresh Look at Marketing," manuscript, 1990.

_____ "Communication in Business: Text, Cases and Glossary," manuscript, 1991.

_____ *Business Innovation and Competitiveness in the Developing World* (Aldershot, England: Avebury, 1993).

_____ *Success in Managing a Small Business* (Aldershot, England:

Avebury, 1994).

_____ *Dimensions of Marketing Management* (Lusaka, Zambia: Zambia Educational Publishing House, 1996).

_____ *Tips for Entrepreneurs* (Toronto, Canada: Productive Publications, 1998).

_____ *Self-Employment: Secrets to Success* (Johannesburg, South Africa: Witwatersrand University Press, 1999).

Lee, S.M. and Schwendiman, G., editors, *Japanese Management: Cultural and Environmental Considerations* (New York: Praeger Publishers, 1982).

Lynch, R.L. et al., *Introduction to Marketing* (New York: McGraw-Hill Book Company, 1984).

Mackenzie, A., *The Time Trap* (New York: American Management Association, 1990).

Marks, J., "Time Out," *U.S. News and World Report*, December 11, 1995.

Maslow, A.H., *Motivation and Personality* (New York: Harper and Brothers Publishers, 1954).

Mayer, J.J., *Time Management for Dummies* (Foster City, CA: IDG Books Worldwide, Inc., 1995).

McCarthy, J.E., *Essentials of Marketing* (Homewood, Illinois: Richard D. Irwin, Inc., 1979).

McCay, J.T., *The Management of Time* (Englewood Cliffs, New Jersey: Prentice-Hall, Inc., 1959).

McGregor, D., *The Human Side of Enterprise* (New York: McGraw-

Hill Book Company, Inc., 1960).

Mills, D.Q., *Labour-Management Relations* (New York: McGraw-Hill Book Company, 1978).

Mintzberg, H., *The Nature of Managerial Work* (Englewood Cliffs, New Jersey: Prentice-Hall, Inc., 1980).

Mitchell, A., "Firms Back Marketing's About-Turn," *British Journal of Marketing*, September 15, 1988.

_____ "The Consumer is No Longer King," *British Journal of Marketing*, September 15, 1988.

Newman, W.H., editor, *Managers for the Year 2000* (Englewood Cliffs, New Jersey: Prentice-Hall, Inc., 1978).

Nwokoye, N.G., *Modern Marketing for Nigeria* (London: The McMillan Press Limited, 1981).

O'Toole, J., *Vanguard Management: Redesigning the Corporate Future* (New York: Berkley Books, 1985).

Ouchi, W.G., *Theory Z: How American Business Can Meet the Japanese Challenge* (Reading, Massachusetts: Addison-Wesley Publishing Company, 1981).

Peter, L.J. and Hull, R., *The Peter Principle: Why Things Always Go Wrong* (New York: William Morrow, 1969).

Peters, T.J. and Waterman, R.H., *In Search of Excellence: Lessons from America's Best-Run Companies* (New York: Harper and Row, 1982).

Pride, W.M. and Ferrell, O.C., *Marketing: Basic Concepts and Decisions* (Boston: Houghton Mifflin Company, 1977).

Pride, W.M. and Ferrell, O.C., *Marketing: Basic Concepts and Decisions*, Fifth Edition (Dallas, Texas: Houghton Mifflin Company, 1987).

Pritchett, P., *New Work Habits for a Radically Changing World* (Dallas, Texas: Pritchett and Associates, Inc., 1996).

_____ *Mindshift: The Employee Handbook for Understanding the Changing World of Work* (Dallas, Texas: Pritchett and Associates, Inc., 1996).

Rapp, S. and Collins, T., *The Great Marketing Turnaround: The Age of the Individual - and How to Profit from It* (Englewood Cliffs, New Jersey: Prentice-Hall, Inc., 1990).

Reddin, W.J., *Managerial Effectiveness* (New York: McGraw-Hill Book Company, 1970).

Rees, W.D., *The Skills of Management* (London: Croom Helm Australia Pty Limited, 1984).

Reinecke, J.A. et al., *Introduction to Business: A Contemporary View* (Boston: Allyn and Bacon, 1989).

Rewoldt, S.H. et al., *Introduction to Marketing Management: Text and Cases* (Homewood, Illinois: Richard D. Irwin, Inc., 1981).

Rosenberg, L.J., *Marketing* (Englewood Cliffs, New Jersey: Prentice-Hall, Inc., 1977).

Ross, J.E., *Productivity, People, and Profits* (Reston, Virginia: Reston Publishing Company, 1981).

Rugman, A.M., et al., *International Business: Firm and Environment* (New York: McGraw-Hill Book Company, 1985).

Schwartz, D.L., *Marketing Today: A Basic Approach* (New York:

Harcourt Brace Jovanovich, Inc., 1981).

Schwartz, D. J., *Marketing Today* (New York: Harcourt Brace Jovanovich, Inc., 1981).

Scott, C.D. and Jaffe, D.T., *Managing Change at Work: Leading
People through Organisational Transitions*, Revised Edition
(Menlo Park, California: Crisp Publications, Inc., 1995).

Seidman, L.W. and Skancke, S.T., *Productivity, the American
Advantage: How 50 U.S. Companies are Regaining the
Competitive Edge* (New York: Simon and Schuster, Inc.,
1990).

Sigband, N.B., *Communication for Management and Business* (Glen-
view, Illinois: Scott, Foresman and Company, 1976).

Stanton, W.J., *Fundamentals of Marketing* (New York: McGraw-Hill
Book Company, 1989).

Steckmest, F.W., *Corporate Performance: The Key to Public Trust*
(New York: McGraw-Hill Book Company, 1982).

Still, R.R. and Cundiff, E.W., *Essentials of Marketing* (Englewood
Cliffs, New Jersey: Prentice-Hall, Inc., 1970).

Stone, F.M. and Sachs, R.T., *The High-Value Manager: Developing
the Core Competencies Your Organisation Demands* (New
York: American Management Association, 1995).

Taylor, F.W., *Scientific Management* (New York: Harper and Brothers, 1947).

Thompson, A.A. and Strickland, A.J., *Strategic Management: Concepts and Cases* (Homewood, Illinois: Richard D. Irwin, Inc.,
1992).

Toffler, A., *Future Shock* (New York: Bantam Books, Inc., 1970).

Tosi, H.L. and Carroll, S.J., *Management* (New York: John Wiley and Sons, 1982).

Vroom, V.H., *Work and Motivation* (New York: John Wiley and Sons, Inc., 1964).

Whitehill, A.M., *Japanese Management: Tradition and Transition* (London: Routledge, 1991).

Whiteman-Jones, M., "Hiring and Keeping the Best: The 10 Commandments," *Colorado Business*, October 1993.

<>

# INDEX

<><

## The Author

**HENRY KYAMBALESA** has worked as a tenured lecturer in Business Administration in the School of Business at the Copperbelt University in Zambia, where he has also held adjunct positions as Assistant Dean and Careers Counsellor and Placement Officer. He has also worked as a salaries accountant and as an Examining Officer in Zambia's Ministry of Finance and the Department of Customs and Excise, respectively.

He earned the B.B.A. degree from the University of Zambia, the M.B.A. degree from Oklahoma City University, and the M.A. degree in International Studies (including the fields of International Business, International Economics, and International Technology Analysis and Management) from the University of Denver. He is currently pursuing a doctoral degree in Management in the U.S.A.

He is the author of the following books: *Business and Social Demands* (Lusaka, Zambia: Zambia Printing Company Publications, 1990); *Business Innovation and Competitiveness in the Developing World* (Brookfield, Vermont, USA: Ashgate Publishing Company, 1993); *Success in Managing a Small Business* (Aldershot, England: Avebury, 1994); *Quotations of Zambian Origin* (Lusaka, Zambia: Apple Books, 1994); *Dimensions of Marketing Management* (Lusaka, Zambia: Zambia Educational Publishing House, 1997); *Tips for Entrepreneurs* (Toronto, Canada: Productive Publications, 1998); and three forthcoming books entitled *Self-Employment: Secrets to Success* (Johannesburg, South Africa: Witwatersrand University Press, 1999), "Marketing in the 21st Century: Text and Glossary," and "Socio-Economic Development in LDCs: Challenges and Imperatives in the 21st Century."

175

For Product Safety Concerns and Information please contact our EU
representative GPSR@taylorandfrancis.com Taylor & Francis Verlag GmbH,
Kaufingerstraße 24, 80331 München, Germany


Printed and bound by CPI Group (UK) Ltd, Croydon, CR0 4YY
01/05/2025
01858327-0001